HIDDEN HISTORY

HISTORY

of

TACOMA

*Little-Known Tales
from the City of Destiny*

———◆———

KARLA STOVER

THE
History
PRESS

Published by The History Press
Charleston, SC 29403
www.historypress.net

First published 2012

ISBN 978-1-5402-0661-9

Stover, Karla Wakefield.
Hidden history of Tacoma : little-known tales from the city of destiny / Karla
Stover.
p. cm.
Includes bibliographical references.
ISBN 978-1-5402-0661-9
1. Tacoma (Wash.)--History--Anecdotes. 2. Tacoma (Wash.)--Social life and
customs--Anecdotes. 3. Tacoma (Wash.)--Biography--Anecdotes. 4. Historic
buildings--Washington (State)--Tacoma--Anecdotes. 5. Tacoma (Wash.)--
Buildings, structures, etc.--Anecdotes. I. Title.
F899.T2S77 2012
979.7'788--dc23
2012000249

To my husband, Ed,
forever the wind beneath my wings,

and my parents,
who told me stories about the old days.

Contents

CONTENTS

Part I

God Made the World and Men Made Tacoma

Just Give the Man a Ruler: Laying Out a Town

The Tacoma Land Company has begun selling lots on what they call Pacific Avenue where they hope a downtown will develop. Two hundred and fifty dollars will buy you a lot with a corner. Non-corner lots go for two hundred dollars. Rental property is one dollar a frontal foot. The land has been burned off but stumps and piles of debris remain. The hill is so water-soaked that the railroad could be trying to build a city in the shallowest lake or steepest swamp known to man.
—an Oregon observer

On September 10, 1873, the Northern Pacific Railroad's board of directors chose Tacoma as the railroad's western terminus. Soon after this, the company purchased three thousand acres of land, including that on which the city is located. The railroad company kept some acreage for railroad shops and depot buildings and assigned to its subsidiary, the Tacoma Land Company, the task of selling the rest.

Laying out cities in the 1870s was child's play. The ideal was a broad rectangle subdivided into squares. All that was required was a map and a ruler. James Tilton, who had been surveyor general of the territory back in the Isaac Stevens era, was still around. The Land Company handed him a ruler and asked him to start drawing.

One story going around at the time was that General Morton Mathew McCarver suggested Tilton follow the plan that had been used to plat Sacramento. Another was that Tacoma's layout was patterned after that of Melbourne, Australia.

Tilton's sketches didn't survive, but on October 3, 1873, in a *Weekly Pacific Tribune* article, he said he just made a few modifications to the basic grid plan then in vogue. He drew three main avenues 100 feet wide to parallel the waterfront and two others slanting diagonally up the face of the hill. The slant was a concession to the difficulties both horse-drawn streetcars and pedestrians would encounter on a direct climb. He flanked these five streets with blocks 120 feet deep. Additional streets for future residential areas were 40 feet wide—too broad to degenerate into alleys but not grand enough to detract from the designated thoroughfares.

He left open a twenty-seven-acre area of land approximately one thousand feet south of the bay for development as a central park or as the campus for a complex of buildings should Tacoma become the county seat or territorial capital. And finally, he left land at both the north and south ends of town for two smaller parks.

This first dream of how Tacoma would look failed to get off the drawing board. Though board members expressed some dissatisfaction with Tilton's proposals for solving drainage problems on the clay-bank hill, far more important was financier Jay Cooke's slide into bankruptcy. As Cooke's railroad bond sales slowed, whatever money the Land Company could raise offered the best hope for working capital. The railroad's directors chose C.B. Wright to head the Land Company, and almost immediately President Wright began to discuss replacing Tilton. Wright wanted the future city platted by the country's best-known landscape architect, the brilliant, unorthodox, opinionated and highly controversial Frederick Law Olmsted.

A journalist turned planner/administrator, Olmsted was most well known for conceiving and bringing into being New York's Central Park. And Olmsted liked "gracefully-curved lines, generous spaces and the absence of sharp corners, the idea being to suggest and imply leisure, contemplativeness, and happy tranquility."

The thought that Wright and the board were concerned with prompting happy tranquility at their terminus is a stretch. What more likely appealed to them was Olmsted's capacity for attracting attention, and his reputation for finding novel solutions to difficult problems of terrain. Whatever their reason, the board summoned Olmsted to the railroad's New York headquarters the day after Cooke's bank closed and commissioned him to make "in all possible haste" a preliminary study for the town site.

Olmsted teamed with G.K. Radford, an experienced sanitary and hydraulic engineer, in creating the plan. How the two men divided the labor isn't known, but it is likely that Radford concentrated on drainage problems and Olmsted on creating a town that would "blend with sea, forest, and mountain." Olmsted never actually came to Tacoma; he worked from contour maps and sketches. His final design featured a meandering latticework of diagonals that climbed the hill from the bay. The plan was delivered to the Northern Pacific on schedule in early December and reached Tacoma the week before Christmas. Tacoma Land Office officials immediately put it on display.

The Land Company building was one of the first in New Tacoma. It was at Ninth Street and Pacific Avenue and was built on pilings over a skunk cabbage swamp. The site was chosen because building over a swamp meant the men didn't have to fell trees and clear a lot. Almost immediately, the company had acres of adjacent woodland slashed down. Thirty-foot-deep piles of wood covered a 480-acre tract, and when the weather was warm enough, the piles were burned. Initially, Tacoma's town site was a smoking ash heap with stumps and a few logs.

Meanwhile, residents, who had been eagerly awaiting the metamorphosis of the clay cliff into the metropolis of their dreams, studied Olmsted's vision with consternation.

Tacoma Land Office, 1874.

An old homestead.

Thomas Prosch, who had bought the Olympia newspaper *Pacific Tribune* from his father, Charles, and moved it to Tacoma on the strength of its prospects as a terminus, reflected the ambivalence of the locals in a long but subdued story that appeared on December 23.

The plan, he said, was "unlike that of any other city in the world" and "so novel in character that those who have seen it hardly know whether or not to admire it, while they are far from prepared to condemn it." The most peculiar features, he wrote,

> *were the varying sizes and shapes of the blocks, and the absence of straight lines and right angles. Every block, street and avenue was curved. The lots had uniform frontages of twenty-five feet, but differed in length. The curvature of the blocks did away with corner lots, and the varying lengths eliminated many of the problems that occurred when people crossed street at corners where collisions and accidents most frequently happen—corners that because of their frequent use resulted in problems with mud and dust.*

Olmsted's three main avenues were Pacific, Tacoma and Cliff, which is now Stadium Way. He designated Pacific Avenue, which came up the bank from the railroad dock and out into the country, for businesses. Two-mile-long Cliff Avenue, which ran along the edge of the bluff, was the residential street. And one-mile-long Tacoma Avenue, which intersected with Pacific Avenue before extending to the water at a spot between Old and New Tacoma, seemed to have no particular designation other than that it would pass the seven parks of varying size Olmsted's plan allowed for. Mr. Prosch felt that time alone would prove the plan's practicality but added, hesitantly, "Certainly, if a large city is ever built here, after that plan, it will be through and through like a park, and have very many important advantages over other cities."

Newspapers in Portland, New Tacoma's main rival at the time, also took a look at Olmsted's plan. The *Bulletin* conceded the originality of the famous planner's concept but noted, "Tacoma is already set upon a hill, or two hills for that matter; it would be ridiculous for such a city to copy after places like Chicago or San Francisco. Tacoma resolves to have individuality and to assert it." The paper also noted that the curve, the favorite geometrical line at Tacoma, was supposedly "borrowed from the movements of the celestial spheres, or other aspects of nature. With these movements," the paper concluded, "Tacoma was determined to be in harmony, and with her new plat, would be almost as perfect as anything can be in this ill-favored world."

Tacomans were neither amused nor enthusiastic about Olmsted's plan. The *Pacific Tribune* had a follow-up story and focused on the "assumed wisdom" of the managers of the Pacific Division of the Northern Pacific rather than on the plan itself. The paper agreed that the Olmsted concept was approved by men of "ripe judgment and unquestioned taste whose views were that it would make a beautiful city and was adapted to the character of the ground." However, many in Tacoma were skeptical. Speculators who wanted to buy corner lots saw no merit in a downtown deliberately left deficient in four-way intersections. To them, Olmsted's dream of a business district without bottlenecks was a nightmare. Nor were the engineering crews assigned to run lines amid downtown's many stumps in order to locate Pacific, Cliff and Tacoma Avenues persuaded by Olmsted's dictum that "speed of traffic is of less importance than comfort and convenience of movement."

Early settlers, who had seen others profit from the rise of foursquare business districts, grumbled that the plan resembled "a basket of melons, peas and sweet potatoes." They said that "in the street patterns one could find representations of everything that has ever been exhibited in an agricultural show, from calabashes to iceboxes."

In prosperous times the Olmsted plan might have survived, even benefited from the controversy and ridicule. But the Northern Pacific's board lacked the confidence to wait out the discontent. Also, after Jay Cooke's bank failed, the financial panic deepened into depression, and the railroad was desperate for capital.

Only forty-three days after he had submitted the plan, Olmsted was notified that his ideas would not be used and his services were no longer required; Tacoma would be built on a traditional grid. Neither the letters of dismissal nor Olmsted's reply have ever been located. And Olmsted did not publically mention the rejection.

As people started buying lots, one of Tacoma's most successful real estate investors was a man named Peter Irving. In 1874, he spent $400 and bought lots at 909 and 911 Pacific Avenue. In 1882, he built two buildings at a cost of $1,500. From then on, tenants made and paid for all the improvements and repairs. For the next twenty-three years, one building was vacant for a month and the other was constantly rented. Generally, the rents were $200 to $225. After the original cost, all taxes and insurance, Mr. Irving netted a profit of between $40,000 and $50,000. In 1905, he turned down an offer of $40,000 for the property and then a second one of $45,000. Instead, he took down the wooden buildings and replaced them with a single brick one. The new building was 16 by 120 feet and had three floors and skylights. It's still in existence, and most old-timers will know it as the building where Ghilarducci's florist used to be.

Not long after the Land Company constructed its little cabin, the Squire Building at 726 Pacific Avenue became Tacoma's first frame building. North School, built at 246 St. Helen's, soon followed. William J. Fife, who moved to

A typical stump house.

New Tacoma with his family in 1874, said he went to school for two years in a dugout with six other pupils because that was all the town could afford.

As 1875 drew to a close, quite a little settlement had developed. Seventy people lived in town; two families lived in the suburbs, and thirteen people lived down on the wharf. A wagon road connected New Tacoma and Old Tacoma. Steilacoom was the county seat, and land office employee Colonel C.P. Ferry had to make frequent trips there to take care of things such as taxes. The easiest way to get to Steilacoom was by wagon or horseback on an old road that went from New Tacoma to Old Tacoma and doubled back close to New Tacoma on the other side of a substantial wooded hill. Colonel Ferry finally persuaded officials to let him use some of New Tacoma's tax revenues to build a shortcut up from Pacific Avenue, creating what is now Ninth Street. The officials allotted thirty-six dollars, which was only enough to slash the road and cut the logs into lengths. New Tacoma residents finished the job. The city's three businesses—a livery stable, store and the land office—shut down for the day, and everyone turned out to clear the road. The work took two days and was followed by a big picnic with lots of speeches. The new road intersected the Old Tacoma–Steilacoom road at about where Division and Ainsworth now meet.

New Tacoma soon had two other buildings. The Washington House, believed to be Tacoma's first hotel, was built at 700 Pacific Avenue in 1875 by a Mr. Fairhurst. In spite of being called a hotel, it was mainly a lodging house for men the Land Company hired to grade roads and lots. The other building was the American Hotel at 702 Pacific Avenue. Both were destroyed by fire.

But the Tacoma Land Company wasn't the only real estate office in town. Its competition was First Real Estate, located in a plain frame building with pine fixtures, owned by Samuel Wilkeson. Mr. Wilkeson was the son of the Northern Pacific board's secretary. In addition to the real estate office, he owned additional downtown property, part of which was at Ninth and Pacific. Before the Rust Building was built there, Mr. Wilkeson built structures that lasted for years. His home, which was considered a city mansion at the time, was at Seventh and Broadway. He also owned much of the property on which Stadium High School now stands.

At some point in the 1880s, the Land Company moved to the Viant and Pierce Building at 728–30 Pacific Avenue. Currently, it's on South Union. And finally, apropos of nothing but an interesting footnote to Tacoma as it used to be, when Commencement Bay was at high tide, the water came clear up to where the Union Depot now stands.

PERIL WITH PILING WORMS: LIFE ON THE WHARF

One day in 1890, a fisherman named Casper Witt, whom papers called "large and fleshy," was walking down Second Street when his leg seemed to collapse under him. He fell onto the sidewalk, and several people rushed to his aid. They were horrified to see what appeared to be pieces of bone protruding through the fabric of his pants.

"Who shot you?" someone shouted.

"Shot, hell!" snapped Casper.

Apparently, Casper had made a fishing haul and, along with other men, brought his catch to shore. As was the custom, he immediately cleaned his nets. Casper wore a rubber boot on one foot, but the other leg was wooden.

"It's them cussed teredoes [piling worms]," he said. I might have known they'd get to work on me. There's a forty-dollar wooden leg gone to smash."

Civilization may have been making its mark on Puget Sound, but Mother Nature had her own ways to strike back.

After Nicholas Delin built a mill on Commencement Bay but left during the Indian Wars and Job Carr arrived ten years later and settled in Old Town, Civil War veteran William Blackwell and his wife, Alice, came with the Northern Pacific Railroad to run a hotel on the wharf. They were instrumental in building Tacoma.

The Blackwells left Kalama on November 15, 1873, spent the night at Tenino and reached Tacoma on the evening of the following day aboard the first passenger train to Tacoma. Railroad employee General John W. Sprague met them at the edge of Commencement Bay below Fifteenth and A Streets, where the tracks stopped, and led them to a boat; several Chinese men then rowed them to the hotel below where Stadium Bowl is today. The tide was out, but men laid planks on the beach, and the couple picked their way up them. The hotel was on a dock built on pilings, so they climbed more planks to the dock.

Their new home and place of business was a covered frame with floors and partitions for the rooms, of which only two were finished. The Blackwells had no food, no place to buy any and no place to cook if they could find some. A man operating a pile driver invited them to dinner and breakfast the following morning, and William hired two railroad workers to return to the

The wharf. *Courtesy of Robin Paterson.*

train and bring back their bedding. Over the next two months, some railroad employees finished the hotel, and others extended tracks there. Both train and hotel business officially began on January 1, 1874.

The Northern Pacific Hotel and the Blackwells' private apartment were on the second floor of the building, which was twenty feet wide and two hundred feet long. William Blackwell and railroad officials had their offices on the ground floor. The hotel had forty bedrooms, some single and some double, and in a pinch slept one hundred. There were two bathrooms, a dining room and a bar. The bartender, Jacob Mann, maintained a two-drink maximum. Chinese men did all the cooking, and Alice Blackwell and one Chinese helper took care of the rooms. After a few years, because of vibrations when ships docked, the building was moved off the pilings and onto land close to the bluff.

As the hotel developed, Alice had hundreds of flower boxes made. At the end of their workday, railroad employees carried back sacks of dirt and leaf mold to fill them. She also bought property in her own name on the hill above the hotel. At the end of her workday, she climbed the hill to her property and took care of her roses and chickens. Until her death, Mrs. Blackwell provided flowers for every important event and to every important visitor who came to Tacoma.

Within a matter of months after their arrival, the Blackwells acquired neighbors. In addition to the railroad officials, there were three families; two small stores; a telegraph office that had been on a floating barge but relocated to a permanent facility; Mr. and Mrs. M.V. Money's combination printing business, newspaper, stationery store and aviary; and Mr. Doughtery's shoe shop. Mr. Dougherty found a three-foot-wide space between two buildings, roofed it and began repairing and making shoes there. The Moneys did all the printing for the local railroad officers—at least for a while. Mrs. Money was very popular with sailors because she ran the shop with a parrot on her head. But after a few years, General Sprague said he was tired of finding parrot tracks on his stationery and, as soon as another printer showed up, took his business elsewhere. Finally, at the far end of the wharf, down near Twenty-first Street, Robert Scott had a dairy. He delivered milk by scow or by wagon, which he decked out with bells, and for additional income he toted visitors around. Tacoma had a shortage of coins, so to supplement them people used brass coins made at the Hanson and Ackerson Mill. The mill's blacksmith hammered out the slugs in three denominations: one dollar, forty-five cents and forty cents. They were intended for use at the company store but soon became accepted currency around town. Mr. Hanson credited residents' honesty, plus the fact that for a time he employed the only blacksmith, for the system's success.

As it continued to develop, the wharf wasn't always a safe place. Part of the land behind it and directly below the bluff was divided into corrals from which animals regularly escaped. One day, a bull got loose, raced through a freight house, gored a horse and two men and disappeared. Another time, it was a flock of sheep. One man walked off the edge of the wharf and fell into the water, and another fellow froze to death in his shack. When the body of a third man was found floating in the bay, it was left all day because Tacoma's limited legal structure had no provisions for the unclaimed dead.

Farmers came by horse and wagon to deliver produce to waiting ships, and merchants picked up goods and staples from the various warehouses. But their horses were known to bolt and upset their wagons. Trains transported coal from the foothills of Mount Rainier and wheat from eastern Washington. However, at least once, a warehouse collapsed under the sheer weight of the wheat it held. In 1894, a strip of land approximately 250 feet long and 50 feet wide slid into the bay, taking with it the home and freight house belonging to H.H. Alger. And the teredoes continued to wreak havoc with peoples' lives. An unnamed young lady slipped into an unexpected hole when a piece of planking gave way and nearly broke her leg.

Nothing in New Tacoma was easy, but it was a vibrant, exciting place, and until the financial panic of the 1890s, opportunities made men rich.

God Made the World and Men Made Tacoma

WATER, WATER EVERYWHERE, BUT NOT A DROP TO DRINK

In 1874, Tacoma was a hamlet of three hundred or so people on Commencement Bay—a cluster of shacks, tents, lean-tos and a few businesses bunched together on the waterfront at the south end of Pacific Avenue—a Pacific Northwest town where, in spite of the rain, water for home use was a major problem.

Springs did trickle out of the hills on the west side of Broadway, and several Chinese families created irrigation systems for a laundry and for vegetable gardens that extended up St. Helens Avenue. However, in those early days, a man named Tom Quan hauled drinking water in a wagon pulled by a mule, Long Ear Nellie, and sold it around town. Then, William Fife built several earthen reservoirs in the vicinity of Ninth and Market Streets. He ordered bored pipes (hollowed-out logs) from Olympia and promised the women of Tacoma that they'd soon have water for Monday morning washday. When water did start filling the pipes, most of it went to put out a fire at the Godkin & Durr Furniture Store. Mr. Fife attached a hose to a faucet, and that helped the bucket brigade, but it was a jerry-rigged system at best. And Tacoma housewives had to wait four more years before all the pipes were laid.

As the 1880s approached, Tacoma had outgrown Mr. Fife's system, and in 1883 two men, John Burns and Philip Metzler, dug into the hill underneath Mr. Burns's house at 945 Market Street. They drove a tunnel, tapped into a number of springs and built a flume that was 350 feet long and 3½ by 7 feet in circumference. The flume ran diagonally across an alley, across another lot and over Market Street, bent a few feet north and emptied into a reservoir. The 100,000-gallon-capacity reservoir was 10 feet deep and 23 by 26 feet above ground. A four-inch "main" came out of it and was laid across various nearby lots on its way down to Pacific Avenue. When it reached Pacific, the flume headed south toward Tenth Street, gradually changing and narrowing from a two-inch wooden pipe to a one-inch galvanized pipe as it reached its end near Ninth Street. Other wooden pipes of varying sizes carried water on to Fourteenth Street with a branch at Twelfth Street over to A Street. The pathetic system was described as one of "puny little arteries."

This crude system, known as the Burns & Metzler Water Plan, was still under construction when, in June 1884, city council members began negotiations with Charles Wright, Tacoma's major patron.

Mr. Wright also owned a water company in Tacoma. He had built two dams in local gullies that were fed by Gallagher's Creek and a reservoir 260

17

feet above sea level and supplemented the creek water with water that came from Spanaway Lake. Gravity fed water to homes and businesses downhill, and a Holly turbine and wheel pump forced water to the higher elevations. By December 1884, water mains had been distributed through the town. On the seventeenth of that month, the Tacoma Hotel was the first to get service, thus making the occasion AN EVENT.

Five years later, Charles Wright visited Tacoma and told a reporter he had no interest in selling his water company to "men who haven't the interest of the city at heart." However, his system wasn't very clean. "Pure Water Snakes!" was the *Tacoma Daily News'* headline.

In May 1891, Deacon Rancipher found and put on exhibition thread-like worms belonging to the *Gordius* family that he'd discovered in the city's drinking water. The horrified reading public was told that the worms ran from six to eighteen inches long; that when divided into segments, each segment grew a head and became its own entity; and that if dried, they would live for three years and revive themselves when put back in fresh water.

Following this disclosure, a *Daily News* reporter went to the home of Reverend W.B. McMillan at 1926 J Street and was shown water samples taken from a neighborhood fire hydrant. Not only did the water have the worms, but it also contained several other aquatic entities all clearly visible with a microscope. Mrs. McMillan was straining her water through muslin. And local vegetarians were warned about what they were eating when they were drinking the water.

By 1892, Charles Wright had changed his mind about selling. His system was proving to be a cash hog. Negotiations between the city and Mr. Wright dragged on until 1893. He finally sold out for $1.75 million.

Unfortunately, no one had checked out the newly acquired system's infrastructure. It was, in fact, falling apart. Tacoma's downtown business district had suffered from four serious leaks, and the flume was so rotten in places that people could push holes in it with a finger. The city engineer estimated that the flume was losing 1.5 million gallons daily. Worse was a lack of a dependable source. Mr. Wright's promise of 5 million gallons of water a day from Thomas and Patterson Springs was a substantial overestimate.

While residents suffered, men checked out Puyallup's Maplewood Springs, Clover Creek's headwaters, Lake Kapowsin, the Chenius River near Fairfax, Canada Creek near Carbonado and an artesian well on the prairie southwest of town. A man named Fred Plummer filed claims on water from Clear Lake and the Big Mashell River, eliminating both of them. Exasperated city officials sued Charles Wright and won.

Tacoma's drinking water. *Courtesy of Robin Paterson.*

In 1906, Mayor George Wright appointed Harnett Fuller to supervise the sorry little water system, the wells and the gravity lines. Mr. Fuller called the South Tacoma wells "a patchwork of everyone's ideas" and said that the "present water supply was a disgrace to a civilization and a standing menace to the community." He sent two crews to check out the untapped and clean Green River. He also recommended abandoning Clover Creek as a source because ducks were paddling in it, cows wading in it and children frolicking in it. And then Tacoma residents shot themselves in the foot. In 1906, voters decided against a Green River gravity line.

Back at square one, the councilmen found that water from Gallagher's Gulch was fed by "chicken yards and cesspools," and the bottom of the Hood Street Reservoir was coated "with a generous stratum of ooze, disease-laden and of an unholy smell." The *Tacoma Times* blasted the council, and the council formed a committee. The committee came up with a long-range plan; an injunction stopped the plan. A local engineer was elevated to special engineer status, and he sunk wells. The wells provided an abundance of water—until they started to go dry. The city started using water from Maplewood Springs, and the council voted to put the Green River gravity line back on the ballot. This time, voters approved it by a two-to-one margin.

Work on the gravity system took two full years. The job required securing right of ways, fighting injunctions from landowners, digging tunnels, creating a bypass line and building a spillway. Men hacked out several miles of roadway through timber and brush and transported sixty-inch pipes forty-three miles, sometimes having to shoulder the pipes and carry them in. The pipeline crossed the White and Puyallup Rivers. Hugging the land's contours, it went from one hundred to nine hundred feet above sea level. Once, the water pressure blew up a wastewater pipe. A verbal altercation broke out over whether the water should be turned on before a hydrochlorite water purification plant was built. Mayor William Seymour said to wait, but public works commissioner Nicholas Lawson ignored him. On July 12, 1913, all the water valves in Tacoma were opened, and 42 million gallons a day of Green River water flowed into Tacoma. At last, Tacoma's water was clean and safe for everyone—even vegetarians.

A TISKET A TASKET, THE STREETCAR HAS A CASKET: PIONEER CEMETERIES

Thursday, June 11, 1874, Frances Desdemona Coulston, daughter of Mrs. Root, now McNeil, aged nineteen years, five months—In the ground just allotted for a cemetery by the Railroad or town company, being the first burial there.
—Reverend Mr. Bonnell

In the early 1870s, when the Northern Pacific Railroad and Tacoma Land Office were establishing Tacoma, the Land Office donated land for the Prairie Cemetery, the fledging community's first official graveyard. It was situated on a knoll alongside what was known as the South Tacoma Plain. This area eventually became the town of Edison and is now South Tacoma. And the cemetery became the Oakwood Cemetery.

The second person buried was General Morton Matthew McCarver, an advocate for Old Tacoma, and the next burials came as the result of a boating accident. A man named John Croft, an engineer from Black Diamond named Chambers and two boys—John Ralston, age sixteen, and his brother Harry, age eleven—were in a rowboat at the mouth of the Puyallup River when it capsized, and they all drowned.

They would not have been alone during their trip to the graveyard. Daniel Collins, Pierce County's coroner, was so conscientious in his duty that he attended every funeral in the area. Wearing a vest, swallowtail coat and top hat, Mr. Collins ensured that his clients were properly interred. When that was done, he of course lingered on to enjoy the free lunch and liquor that families of the deceased provided.

Adjacent to the Oakwood Cemetery was another little graveyard referred to as either the Pierce County Cemetery or the Paupers' Cemetery. Little is known about it except that the remaining inscriptions suggest it was the final resting place of sailors from foreign ports who died in Tacoma.

In 1881, the Tacoma Land Company donated land at Forty-eighth Street and South Tacoma Way for Old Tacoma Cemetery. Three years later, the land was officially transferred to the city, and a cemetery association was formed. About this time, when there wasn't anything except a blacksmith shop at 4810 South Asotin, a man named R.F. Radebaugh began developing the land around South Fortieth and Forty-first. He built his own estate, which included a pavilion at 6602 South Alaska, and was involved in getting the Tacoma and Puyallup Railway lines extended out to the cemetery. Once completed, streetcar funerals became popular. Rather than chance transporting a coffin to the graveyard by wagon on Tacoma's muddy roads, people loaded the caskets onto streetcars, and all the mourners rode out with it.

Also in 1884, a fellow named A.J. Littlejohn took over land that is now part of both Oakwood and Tacoma Cemeteries, bought more from John Rigney and platted it. Then he started selling lots. Eventually, this led to problems.

By 1905, 205 deceased soldiers resided in Tacoma cemeteries. And by coincidence, Oakwood and Old Tacoma each had the graves of 99 veterans. At Old Tacoma, 92 were Union soldiers from the Civil War, 2 were Confederates and 5 were from other wars. At Oakwood, 95 were Civil War veterans, their various companies not known, and the remaining 4 were from other wars. In May, the *Tacoma Daily News* listed every deceased soldier, where they were buried and the company they served in, if available, and a huge memorial took place. Everyone who could donate flowers left them at various schools, and floral committee members picked them up to distribute. There were speeches and services, and all the remaining veterans who were able participated.

For the next twenty years, Oakwood continued to grow, adding a "crematory" that became a popular option. However, by 1927 the paupers' field was in bad shape. The county's rule was to do the job as cheaply as possible. Pierce County contracted with various undertakers, who, for $4.50, were supposed to provide a wooden box, deliver the body to the cemetery, dig

Casket sealer. *Courtesy of Automatic Wilbert Vault Company, Inc.*

the grave and see to the burial. The contract passed to a different undertaker every three months. According to the *Tacoma Daily Ledger*, diggers sometimes dug holes barely four feet deep, put the coffin in, sprinkled a little dirt over the box and left the rest piled nearby. Blame was twofold: officials were held responsible for the graveyard's unkempt appearance, and the undertakers were responsible for the slipshod burials. After complaints, Commissioner Harry Ball proposed that a new grave site be purchased, and in May 1928, by city ordinance, the old paupers' field was closed.

Old Tacoma Cemetery also had a problem. In 1900, someone discovered that a few of the bodies were buried on the street right of way, an issue that took finesse to resolve.

Many of the grave markers and burial sites at Old Tacoma Cemetery have interesting stories. One tombstone reads, "Here lies the body of Pickhandle Shorter, all as John Davis." The gentleman in question was a longshoreman whose co-workers passed the hat to buy a stone. It was supposed to read "alias John Davis," not "all as." The stonecutter goofed. Another, commemorating a veteran of the California gold rush, reads, "In Days of Old, In days of gold, In days of 49, John W. Kline." Lena Clark was buried in a huge plot with a granite spire indicating that others would one day join her. They didn't. She rests bereft of family. One family plot has three heavy, sunken vaults, the center one containing the body of a girl buried in 1918. Her parents were supposed to be on either side, but her father is buried elsewhere and her mother disappeared. Two nightlife characters are buried close to two women who did their best to keep the sailors away from said nightlife.

And those who know local history will find the graves of a number of the city's major movers and shakers: the Proctors of Proctor Street, Allen C. Mason of Mason Street and School, the Howard Carrs of Carr Street and many others. Cemeteries are places where dead men do tell tales.

Smoke Gets in Your Eyes: 1889, the Year of Fires

In the year 1889, Washington cities burned. Seattle was nearly wiped out in June, Ellensburg in July and Spokane in August. Vancouver, Roslyn and Goldendale also had devastating fires. But some towns seemed to have more fires than others, and Tacoma was one of those.

On May 29, 1880, the New Tacoma Hook-and-Ladder Company No. 1 became Tacoma's first firefighting company. It consisted of a wagon, period. In October, the company fought its first officially noted fire when druggist Walter St. John opened a can of gasoline while holding a candle. His carelessness started an inferno that destroyed both his store and living quarters, leaving St. Johns destitute. The next day, city officials called an emergency meeting and approved the immediate purchase of a water cart and fire hose.

Nine years later, fire department officials were still warning city council members that Tacoma was inadequately prepared to fight anything bigger than a burning match. The fire department had five hand-drawn hose carts, but three were unfit for use. There was a hook-and-ladder truck, but it was out of order. The fire hose was only 2,600 feet long, and a reliable source of water was almost nonexistent.

Faced with these facts, however, the council erred on the side of economy because $6,700 of city funds had already been committed for the purchase of a Gramwell Fire Alarm System. The firefighters pointed out that the alarm might ring, but it didn't much matter if there was no equipment with which to fight the fires—but their comments fell on deaf ears. In fact, if it hadn't been for the massive Seattle fire in June, it is debatable whether council members would ever have taken action. As it was, within days of Seattle's fire, a public meeting was held.

To say that Tacoma residents were upset is an understatement. They blamed Tacoma's fires on lax law enforcement, leniency within the judicial system or "a crazy arsonist running amok in Tacoma and through the state leaving burning towns in his wake."

"You may call it vigilance, Christianity or hell!" shouted one man. "Preservation is the first law of nature. I'll shoot any 'sluzer' found around my house after dark!"

City officials received a petition asking for greater fire protection, steam engines and fifty fire hydrants. The signers also expressed concern about

At ease on the fire wagon.

the availability of water for the hydrants. As a result of the petition, council members approved the purchase of two steam engines and some horses. They also hired full-time, salaried firemen.

Tacomans were beginning to feel a little more secure when, on August 29, a man named John Bell went to a local paint and oil store to buy some "asphaltum," a petroleum residue consisting mainly of hydrocarbons. When he turned the faucet of the drum in which it was stored, fire came out instead. Flames immediately spread across the store's wooden floor, up the walls and onto neighboring buildings. The fire department was alerted, but piles of construction materials in the roads delayed arrival. Once again, downtown Tacoma lost businesses (many of which were uninsured), and the owners had to rebuild.

Once again, the community was highly irate.

Then, a local man named C.P. Ferry suggested fighting fires with salt water. It was, he pointed out, a more reliable source than trying to use water from the various springs that dotted Tacoma's hills. Ferry proposed either a 200,000-gallon wooden tank or a 3-million-gallon reservoir to be built on the hill above the town but connected to a pumping station on the waterfront. He figured the cost would be $100,000, and the community was pretty well convinced of its viability. However, and perhaps just coincidentally, a lecturer named Dr. De Witt Talmage came to the Germania Hall to speak. His topic, "Big Blunders," apparently resonated with the locals. Ferry's plan was dropped.

City officials were doing their part. Toward the end of the year, Tacoma owned four steam engines, four hook-and-ladder trucks, a chemical engine, seven horse-pulled carts and ten horses, a life net, life-preserving belts, electric wire scissors, ten thousand feet of hose and, of course, the Gramwell Fire Alarm System. On December 19, two cottages and the St. James Hotel at South Ninth and Yakima caught fire. The flames broke out at 11:17 p.m., but it was 12:15 a.m. before actual firefighting began. The firemen blamed the water department, and the water department said the firefighters were negligent. As it turned out, the city council was at fault. Imagine its chagrin. Apparently, it had taken delivery of, but never bothered to test, the Gramwell System, and it wasn't functioning properly.

The situation was a case of the city council fiddling while Tacoma burned.

WANDERING GHOSTS AND WATERY GRAVES

Before Old Town became trendy, it was a place of lumber mills and loggers, fishing boats and fishermen and a ghost—or so it was said—a tiny figure with coal black hair and bound feet shod in embroidered shoes. Down the hill she floated, away from the gingerbread house, long since gone, that was her prison, toward a houseboat that only briefly was the home of her heart. Dark and empty, it floated in shafts of moonlight, waiting for its captain and his little Apple Blossom.

One hundred and thirty years ago, all the schoolchildren knew the story of the handsome sea captain who loved the daughter of a Chinese Mandarin. The captain's route regularly took him from Tacoma to Victoria Harbor in Hong Kong. Once there, and after he'd docked and taken care of business, he went to visit the home of a Mandarin. And after dinner, while the old man dozed, the captain and little Apple Blossom trysted in the garden.

One night, she met him with the sad news that she was to be married. As the tears flowed from her beautiful, almond-shaped eyes, the captain picked her up, carried her to his ship and set sail for Tacoma.

The young Chinese bride was happy in Old Tacoma, but her actions had caused both her father and bridegroom to lose face. Their retribution wasn't far behind. One day, the captain came home and found her gone. "Apple Blossom was stolen by a *genji*," the servants said. And search though he might, the captain never found his bride.

One hundred and thirty years ago, the white skeletal remains of a house with glassless windows haunted a hill in Old Tacoma, and passersby, especially schoolchildren, crossed to the other side of the street. Everyone in the neighborhood knew that sometimes, especially at night, a white apparition appeared in the garden, stared with grief out of empty eye sockets and held out tiny hands toward a phantom boat in the harbor that only she could see.

Did she know she wasn't alone?

One hundred and thirty years ago, the land south of Old Tacoma, where the docks remain, was also haunted, and worse: it was cursed. The small beachfront shacks that had once been homes to Indian fishermen were, instead, housing natives dying from white men's diseases. And over the body of his third dead son, one elderly man gazed across Commencement Bay and murmured, "The Great Spirit is angry. The ground is cursed."

The Indian disappeared from history, leaving behind nothing but his prophecy. Forty years later, the hotel that graced the area suddenly caught fire and burned to the ground. Among those gathered to watch the flames,

The crew of the *Andelana, Courtesy of www.jawsmarine.com.*

a few were old enough to remember the prophecy. After the fire, the burned land remained vacant. It was said that sometimes those who ventured far enough into the woods above the beach caught glimpses of ghostly figures and heard the sounds of Indian drums.

Commencement Bay also holds its share of restless dead. Emma Stubbs was only fifteen when, on November 14, 1894, her home on the Northern Pacific Railroad's warehouse pier slid into the bay. There she remained, alone amid the mud and debris, until the evening of January 14, 1899. On that night, the ship *Andelana* and its entire crew disappeared.

The *Andelana* was a four-masted barque launched ten years earlier in Liverpool, England. While at anchor in Tacoma a few hundred yards northeast of the St. Paul and Tacoma Mill's deep-water wharf, the captain had its ballast removed and dropped a three-ton anchor off the starboard side. For additional security, both sides were fastened to heavy logs. The barque was riding the current, pointed in a southerly direction, when a freak windstorm came up. In the heavy gale, the ship rose up, the ballast chains gave way and it toppled over and sank. At dawn, a signal lamp rode the waves, flashing its warning lights where only hours before a fine steel ship had been. Over the next few days, oars, a mattress, a compass and other small articles washed up along a half-mile stretch of shore. Six days after the tragedy, one South Tacoma man posited that the men in the ship were probably still alive, holed up in some airtight compartment, waiting desperately for rescue. But nothing was done. Back then, divers said the spot where the *Andelana* had gone down was too deep for them to make successful descents. Except for one man who had been in the hospital, every member of the crew drowned that night.

The ship has apparently been found from time to time. In 1935, a diver looking for a tugboat's anchor stumbled upon its silt-covered hulk. A year later, some of the ship's ironwood railing was hauled up and made into gavels for Republican clubs around the state, but the wreck has never been explored by divers. And the dead crew members are still there, keeping company with Emma Stubbs.

But perhaps the most bizarre story involving the walking dead occurred in 1958, when three Tacoma people became eligible to inherit a share of the estate of Mrs. Helen Dow Park. Mrs. Park, who had been addicted to Ouija boards since she was nineteen, claimed to have been communicating with the ghost of John Gale Forbes for eighteen years. As a result, she left him money in her will. The Connecticut Supreme Court ruled that a ghost couldn't inherit, and Mr. Forbes's very-much-alive Tacoma relatives were happy to step in on behalf of their deceased relative.

Part II

Anything You Can Do, Tacoma Can Do Better

CATCH IT IF YOU CAN: TURNIP TOSSING FROM THE NATIONAL REALTY BUILDING

On February 27, 1910, a large steel girder being shipped to Tacoma for use in construction of the National Realty Building was lost in transit. The building's frame was several feet tall, and all the other steel pieces were piled up and waiting when the fact of the missing girder was noticed. How something that large could actually be lost was never explained. But it was MIA until March 20, when someone found it in Three Forks, Montana.

Land on Pacific Avenue's east side, between Eleventh and Twelfth Streets, was first developed in April 1883, when the Tacoma Land Company sold lots to a man named A.S. Baker. Mr. Baker paid $1,700 for them and sixteen months later sold the property to Philo S. Mead of McPherson, Kansas, for $10,000. Mr. Mead held on to the land, passing it on to his widow, Alverda, upon his death. When Mrs. Mead sold the lots to the National Realty Company in 1909 for $80,000, its value had increased by 4,600 percent, or 175 percent a year. Checks this size didn't often clear Tacoma banks, and as soon as it was cancelled, the National Realty Company's president, L.W. Pratt, got hold of it and kept it as a souvenir. Interestingly, Mrs. Mead was represented by D.P. Calkins and Mrs. W.H. Gratton of Rae, Calkins & Company. There can't have been many female attorneys in Tacoma in 1909.

At the time of the sale, the property had a wood-frame building. Its occupants were Samuel Wolff's German Bakery; the Pullman Saloon, run by Misters Martin and Boyer, which was an exact replica of the inside of a Pullman railroad car; Ben Klegman's loan office; and a jewelry store. Mr. Klegman vacated immediately. The others were given notice to be out by July 1.

National Realty paid architects Heath and Twitchell $12,500 to draw up plans and brought in a man named John L. Hall from a New York company of structural steel engineers to assist the architects with the details of the steel work. The plans were to be completed by June 1, and the contractors had thirty days to assemble teams so work could start the first of July. It was anticipated that construction would be completed and the building occupied by April 1, 1910. A group of men, including President Pratt, sank test holes on May 24, 1909, to determine the character of the soil where the footings would go, and the president officially broke ground. The total cost of the building was expected to be $350,000.

The National Realty Building, circa 1912.

On October 2, 1909, a concrete retaining wall went up along Pacific, and the next day the first footing forms went in. To get this far, four thousand cubic yards of dirt had to be removed. The steel frame—approximately nine hundred tons of it—started arriving in mid-November.

By November 21, the *Tacoma Daily Ledger* was referring to the building as nineteen stories—8,400 tons of iron, steel, brick, plaster, wood and other things. It was also announced that it would not have what was called a party wall; that is, it wouldn't share walls with adjoining buildings.

Anything You Can Do, Tacoma Can Do Better

According to the paper, even though the footings of a "party line are buried, their existence was known to be impractical, and sometimes involve structure damage that caused litigations." In an excess of information, reporters went into great detail about the new skyscraper's cantilever construction and the numbers of and placement of every concrete footing, steel I-beam and cast-iron base block. Tacoma reporters were nothing if not detailed. This was, they claimed, the tallest such building on the Pacific Coast.

The building opened onto Court A in the back and Pacific Avenue in front. The front was in the French Renaissance style using terra cotta and Roman-style bricks. Over the entrance were life-sized groups of statuary symbolizing agriculture, mining, manufacturing and transportation—Puget Sound's main industries. Above a terra cotta balcony at the fourteenth floor were groups of dormers. The roof was 226 feet above Pacific Avenue and held a 57-foot flagpole.

The basement had a restaurant in front—naturally, reporters referred to it as "one of the finest cafés on the coast"—and the heating and power apparatus in the rear. The first floor had two stores, one each facing Pacific Avenue and Court A. The other floors were all offices—367 of them. There were four elevators enclosed in bronze grillwork and polished wire glass and a main staircase of similar design.

As construction went on, naysayers were claiming the building wasn't needed and that it would become a white elephant. However, President Pratt said that applications for space were coming in.

This was a good time to be a laborer in Tacoma. A carpenter made four dollars a day, and there were plenty of jobs. Unfortunately, a rush of business at eastern steel mills delayed construction crews at National Realty from getting their beams and girders, and the first ones sent were inferior and were rejected. Beginning in December, full crews of structural steelworkers in Tacoma sat largely idle. After the situation with the inferior beams and girders was straightened out, high winds and torrential downpours continued to keep work on hold, and then the situation of the missing girder popped up. Apparently, because of a storm and flood blockade, the railroad stopped all freight shipments over its northern lines—and forgot to let anyone know.

The National Realty Building was finally done in the fall of 1910. According to an ad, all the offices were outside rooms, meaning they had windows. They were finished in marble and mahogany. There were thirty-two marble-lined bathrooms, steam heat and hot and cold water in each office, as well as electric lights, something called direct and alternating current gas, compressed air, four high-speed elevators, a law library and a Cutter mail chute. That's a sort of tube that runs from the top floor to the bottom, with places on each floor in which to drop envelopes. Mailmen emptied the chute at the bottom. The chutes were regularly jammed when someone tried to stuff in an oversized envelope.

Now that the building was completed, the unconventional users appeared. A juggler named Zanetta was first. Zanetta's specialty was standing on a stage and having turnips, which he caught on the tines of a fork, thrown at him from different areas of the theater. To drum up business, his manager claimed that Zanetta could catch a turnip thrown from the tallest building in town. According to the *Times*, the procedure was somewhat dangerous as the veggie picked up considerable force during its fall. Nevertheless, a *Tacoma Times* employee offered $100 if Zanetta could catch the turnip the first time it was thrown from the National Realty Building and $50 if it took two times. The *Times* held the money, and a date and time were set: April 20, 1917, at 1:30. Approximately ten thousand people crowded the streets, windows and roofs to watch. It took Zanetta three times to catch the turnip. He didn't get a cent and disappeared from history. The turnip went on display at Mr. Bonney's Pharmacy.

The next unusual event began seven months later, coincidentally at the same time the Puget Sound State Bank moved into the first floor. Already, some remodeling was deemed necessary. The floor and wainscoting were redone with Alaska marble and the rooms in mahogany with ornamental plaster ceilings. Verde antique marble, Mexican onyx and bronze screens were added, as was a burglarproof safe. After the facelift, a pigpen was installed on the roof. Dr. C. Stuart Wilson had a sty built, and 125 porkers moved in. They were well fed and kept in good physical condition, but Dr. Wilson was the city's pathologist, and they were his guinea pigs. Pigs' blood and organs were considered at the time to be more like that of humans than any other animal. Every day, an assistant took a pig to the doctor's office and inoculated it with water from the Green River or fed it milk, food or various other items to determine if they were safe for human consumption. This went on until the animal died. The experiments cost Tacoma sixty-five cents a day.

In 1915, the pigs were gone, and architect George Gove put a garden on the roof. In a ten- by fifteen-foot space, he planted flower boxes and large jars with verbena, nasturtiums, pansies, begonias and sweet Williams and designed trellises of white lattice and mesh for vine flowers. He watered his plants daily and moved them inside in winter.

Also in 1915, Mr. C.L. Andrews, a local baggage agent for the Milwaukee Railroad, fell down the elevator shaft. According to the elevator operator, Neil Webster, he brought the elevator to a stop and opened the door. When

Andrews stepped out, the cage started up and stopped between the twelfth and thirteenth floors. Andrews had just started out, and he fell from the elevator, hit his head on the floor and fell back into the shaft, falling thirteen floors down. The dead man was only twenty-three.

In 1916, more than twenty local businessmen were busted at an illegal drinking party. One of the building's tenants was the Electric Logging Company, which doubled as a private men's club. The club operated by selling membership cards, a secret signal and keys to potential members at a cost of $2.50. The key admitted the men any time, day or night; the elevators ran until midnight, and a drink cost fifteen cents.

"Jump if you want to, but eleven floors is a long way down," Detective Teale said during the bust when three men rushed to windows.

Newspaper accounts claimed that 350 prominent businessmen and physicians were associated with the company and that the "blind pig" was being held in five rooms behind the legitimate business portion of the office. The police seized eight quarts of whiskey, eighteen bottles of seltzer water and several cases of ginger ale. Proprietor Fred Plugardt was arrested and immediately ratted out bartender Fred Lucas. The names of the "350 prominent businessmen and physicians" were never released.

One had to read between the lines to figure out the building's financial situation. In August 1917, based on its second mortgage, the building was sold to a syndicate composed chiefly of men from eastern Washington. Five weeks later, Jack "the Human Fly" Williams climbed up an outside wall, reaching the roof in an hour and a half. Jack was a former trapeze artist who got his start climbing when he rescued a crippled woman trapped on the fourth floor of a burning building. In Tacoma, the street crowd passed a hat and collected $257.10. Jack gave $64.00 to the Soldiers' and Sailors' Club and kept the rest as his due.

In 1920, the National Realty Building became the Puget Sound National Bank Building. Someone was killed in the elevator shaft, owls nested in the tower and Munsey Gymnasium opened on the fourth floor. Businesses came and went in renovated offices. It remains a symbol of Tacoma's historical, or possibly hysterical, past.

ALL ROADS LEAD TO RHODES

At the end of the nineteenth and the turn of the twentieth century, Tacoma was rich with department stores. Gross Brothers, built in 1889 and demolished

Rhodes Brothers, circa 1911.

to make room for the Pantages Theater, was the first. People Store followed six years later at the southeast corner of Eleventh and Pacific. Stone-Fisher-Lane on the corner of Eleventh and Broadway was built in 1905.

Rhodes Brothers began as Rhodes delivery wagons, with Albert, William, Henry and Charles Rhodes delivering tea and coffee throughout Pierce County and picking up orders for the following week. In 1892, the brothers took over the rooms occupied by the R.S. Albright Company at 938 Broadway. Their stock could have fit in one of their delivery wagons. A year later, the brothers moved into the Warburton Building at 1101–03 Broadway, a building occupied by Owl Drug Company. In 1894, they made yet another move—right across the street. But the moves weren't over yet. After three years on Broadway, the brothers moved to Pacific Avenue, a few doors below Eleventh Street. Not until 1903 did Rhodes Brothers Department Store open at the address most people recall, at 950 Broadway, across from Woolworth.

Anything You Can Do, Tacoma Can Do Better

The first mention of the new store was on January 18, 1903; the grand opening was a mere ten months later, on November 8, 1903. The new Rhodes Brothers department store was modeled after Philadelphia's Wanamaker's and Chicago's Marshall Fields. In recognition of the store's horse-and-buggy days, three old wagon wheels were made into a chandelier and were a fixture—in more ways than one. Other than that, mahogany wood and large plate glass windows were the main features for both the building and the display cases. The new store had three floors, each 12 by 110 feet. A mezzanine between the first and second floors provided wicker chairs in which shoppers could sit and rest, with a lavatory and ladies' lounge on one side and the cashiers' cage, large enough for eight people, on the other. Lawson's cable carriers connected the cashiers to the various departments. An orchestra played continuously during the three days of the opening. After that, a piano player entertained from the gallery.

The first floor was dress goods, men's wear, some domestics, a shoe shop, a candy department and Bargain Square. The entire north side was the tea and coffee department, personally handled by Henry Rhodes. Four "electric grinding mills" operated constantly under the attention of "uniformed nurses." Saturday shoppers received complimentary cups of coffee.

Glass, crockery, china, stoneware and pottery took up most of the second floor. The rest of the space was taken over by infants' wear, a suit department and fitting rooms. A "large force of competent seamstresses" had space on the third floor and handled alterations. They shared the floor with furniture, art and framing and a large basket department. All totaled, the store employed one hundred people, of whom fifteen were deliverymen who made daily deliveries from four delivery wagons or, if necessary, by streetcar. The wagons were replaced with cars in 1912. The clerks were well screened and trained in efficiency and courtesy. The female clerks wore dark dresses with white collars and cuffs in the winter and fall and dark skirts with white blouses in spring and summer. The men dressed in suits.

Thanks to hundreds of signs, most everyone in south-central Puget Sound knew about Tacoma's prestigious new department store. No records remain of when Rhodes Brothers began putting up road signs. It's believed to have been around the turn of the twentieth century. The signs read, "All Roads Lead to Rhodes," and included the number of miles to the store in Tacoma. They were placed throughout southwest Washington as far south as the Columbia River and east to the Grays Harbor area. For many years, they served the same purpose as a yellow line does today. The Rhodes signs were Washington's first highway signs.

Rhodes Brothers was definitely the place for upscale shopping, but to stay on top, Rhodes continually made improvements: in 1905, a sprinkler system; 1907, the first enlargement; 1908, a tearoom; and 1911, a major addition that doubled its size. The dining room was located on the top floor at Rhodes. It sat three hundred people. The tables were covered with white linen tablecloths and napkins and crystal vases holding fresh flowers. Lunch was served every day, and dinner was served one or two nights a week. Favorites on the menu were broiled crab, mulligatawny soup, clam chowder and Rhodes' cheesecake. In 1914, improvements included a rooftop garden. The Roof Garden was located just off the Sixth Floor Tea Room. Lunch was served daily from 11:30 a.m. until 2:00 p.m., afternoon tea was served daily from 2:00 p.m. to 5:15 p.m. and evening dinner was served on Saturdays from 5:30 to 7:00 p.m.

As most women wore hats when they went out, the store included its own millinery department. At that time, store buyers traveled back east once or twice a year to buy "model" hats in the latest fashion. The models were quite expensive and were used by local hat makers to make copies for sale to the public.

One of the department store's most interesting features, though, was its date book. For many years, a lady named Marguerite Darland took care of an appointment register where people could leave messages. Every day, she put fresh paper in the book and set out a supply of sharpened pencils. Wives left word for their husbands about where the car was parked, women left short groceries lists, girls broke dates and shoppers arranged to meet friends. Some notes were in code and others in foreign languages. One squabbling couple left messages that became ever less vitriolic until they eventually made up. Newspapers called it an index of life.

In 1920, the store, in need of more floor space, purchased the Judson Block. They connected it to the main store with a sky bridge and named the addition the Annex.

Henry Rhodes retired in 1925, but that didn't stop the progress. In 1936, Rhodes became one of the few department stores in the country to have a library annex. On the building's sixth floor, a librarian took care of seven thousand books, many about etiquette, gardening, cooking and home making, and answered dozens of questions daily: "How can I test this fabric to see if it is pure silk?" "What would be a good name for our new baby?" "Do you have instructions on how to build a cottage?" When the beleaguered librarian wasn't giving advice about proper hats for a wedding, she was answering questions or finding books for people on banking, finance, salesmanship and any number of other issues.

The store employed a professional window dresser who was expected to be on top of all news and trends. When Weaver studios made *Hearts and Fists* in Tacoma, one window display was of an average living room with assorted camera equipment. When cars became popular and people took to the roads, the latest in luggage was on display.

Another favorite feature at Rhodes was a miniature Milwaukee Railroad train, the Hiawatha. During the Christmas shopping season, children could ride the Hiawatha to the North Pole to visit Santa.

During World War II, the *Saturday Evening Post* made pocket-sized versions of its magazine that were sixty-four pages long. They were called *Post Yarns*—except by the servicemen, who called them dehydrated *Saturday Evening Posts*. *Post Yarns* were available at Rhodes, which also had a special *Post Yarns* mailing center and provided free delivery for the miniature magazine plus a personal note from the sender.

When escalators became the vogue, Rhodes Brothers added them. It provided a parking garage. *Seventeen* magazine sponsored a back-to-school style show at the store. But by the 1970s, the store was making plans to move to the Tacoma Mall. At some point in time, Western Department Stores, Inc., bought Rhodes. Most of the stores became Rhodes Western and were bought by Amfac, but the Tacoma and Lakewood stores were sold to Frederick and Nelson, which went out of business in 1992.

ELEVENTH STREET BRIDGE: THE PREQUEL

When in 1892 the idea of building the first bridge connecting Tacoma and the tide flats was under consideration, not everyone thought it was a good idea. Midwest farmers had experienced several years of drought, which left them short of cash needed to pay their debts; the railroads were overbuilt and overextended; and the Sherman Silver Purchase Act was requiring the government to purchase millions of ounces of silver. Signs pointed to an impending financial panic. Nevertheless, the second reading of an ordinance to call a special election for the issuance of bonds to build the bridge took place on the afternoon of December 3, 1892.

Bank president William Blackwell and businessman E.T. Durgin thought the chosen location was bad. Alexander Parker objected to property owners on the flats paying little or nothing for the bridge when they reaped the majority of the benefits. Colonel J.M. Steel, W.H. Fife and Alexander Parker

Grand Opening

Eleventh Street Bridge

Tacoma, Washington
February 15, 1913

W. W. SEYMOUR	Mayor
OWEN WOODS	Commissioner of Public Works
A. U. MILLS	Commissioner of Public Safety
RAY FREELAND	Commissioner of Finance
N. LAWSON	Commissioner of Light and Water
W. C. RALEIGH	City Engineer
WADDELL AND HARRINGTON	Consulting Engineers

were concerned about the city going into debt that would be passed on to their children, and C.L. Mangum pointed out that the plans he'd seen showed the proposed bridge stopping in five feet of water. "The tide flats should be improved, first" he said. But other businessmen, such as department store owner Abe Gross and Stampede tunnel builder Nelson Bennett, felt differently. The ayes had it, and all the hemming and hawing actually saved Tacoma money. Voters had approved a $115,000 bond with 5 percent interest to be paid the first year. However, as written, the bond failed to include subsequent payments. The first bids received had to be set aside because of legal quibbling. The second bids were also set aside, and by the time the third set of bids came in, the price of steel had dropped substantially. The United States War Department approved a design, and construction began.

Construction began, but the work actually began many years earlier. Territorial governor Isaac Stevens ordered a survey of the Puyallup and Muckleshoot Indian Reservations in the 1850s. The boundaries they established governed how Tacomans could develop land for industry and shipping along Commencement Bay's south shore and within the Puyallup delta.

When the Northern Pacific Railroad came, it determined waterfront development because the railroad owned and/or controlled all of the bay's south shore on into the Thea Foss Waterway. The railroad's subsidiary company, the Tacoma Land Company, had been trying to buy the Puyallup Indians' tidelands for $2.50 an acre. Land patents were issued to the Indians on January 30, 1886, and filed in Tacoma/Pierce County on March 20. The Dawes Act, adopted by Congress in 1887, authorized the president of the United States to survey tribal land and divide it into allotments for individual Indians. However, the secretary of the interior was holding back delivery of the patents, so a Tacoma man named Frank C. Ross wrote to President Grover Cleveland, who had just been sworn in. Almost immediately, the Indians received their deeds.

Back then, all the tide and hill lands as far south as the old Chicago, Milwaukee & St. Paul Railroad yard's ocean terminal was in King County. Three men—Puyallup Indian Jerry Meeker, Fremont Campbell and Frank Ross—thought that the land should be in Pierce County. So Mr. Meeker got the Indians to sign a petition requesting the annexation, which they presented to members of the state legislature. The members approved it unanimously, and Governor John Rogers signed the bill on January 10, 1901. Realizing they'd been snookered, King County went to the legislature and had a bill passed to the effect that in the future a change of annexation would require the approval of the majority of county voters, not just those in a particular neighborhood. But for the tide flats, the damage was done as far as King County was concerned.

With that taken care of, Jerry Meeker then got the Indians to sign quitclaim deeds on the property adjoining the state tidelands east of the Puyallup River, and that gave Frank Ross the right to buy the tidelands from the state. Mr. Ross then hired Walter M. Bosworth from the Oregon firm of Ogden and Bosworth to survey East Eleventh Street from A Street across the state tidelands as far as the bluff on the west side, being sure to keep on state land only. Governor engineers had put in four- by four-foot stakes painted white to designate the locations of the Indians' land. Mr. Ross had Mr. Bosworth put in a stone monument near East Eleventh and Taylor Way because he was afraid that during a high tide, and with water rushing into the river, a log would knock out the stakes. All his work was instrumental in Tacoma's ability to construct the first Eleventh Street Bridge.

Two issues the first bridge had to consider were the approaches. On the west side, engineers built a 340-foot-long iron viaduct—a viaduct is a bridge composed of several small spans—with one plate girder span of 60 feet and one of 64 feet. The drop in elevation on the east approach was resolved via a pile trestle. The St. Paul and Tacoma Lumber Company, which was instrumental in getting the bridge built, got the contract to make the trestles. The bridge itself had 6-foot-wide sidewalks, two fixed spans of 185 feet each and a draw span of 250 feet. A Bowers dredge in the channel excavated a spot for a pivotal pier for a drawbridge. Two hoisting engines, chains, pulleys, hawsers and a gang of from twenty to thirty men maneuvered eight-ton, sixty-foot girders into place all under the supervision of crowds of people standing on the bluff.

The total cost of the first Eleventh Street Bridge was $100,000, and it lasted for thirteen years. In 1913, when it had to be replaced, not a few people claimed that city neglect made the new bridge necessary.

GIRDER TO GOD ON THE RUST BUILDING

When Dr. Samuel A. Ambrose needed a larger facility where he could treat patients using "radio vitant rays, spinal concussors, hydro-therapy, solar arc rays" and other non-drug methods, he moved the Ambrose Physiological Clinic, his burgeoning medical practice, into the newly completed Rust Building. As it

The Rust Building, circa 1924.

turned out, he soon outgrew his twelve-room suite there and built his own clinic, but the Rust Building had plenty of other tenants to take his place.

Construction on the Rust Building, known between 1929 and 1931 as the Townsend Building and occasionally as Seafirst Center, began in 1919. Not long before that, Olympia's Temple of Justice had been successfully built from Wilkeson sandstone, so owner William Rust and his architect chose the same material. It was the first office building in the United States to use the local material.

Unlike other Tacoma buildings, the newspapers were more interested in who the tenants would be than in particulars of the construction. Lundquist-Lilly, whose labeled merchandise occasionally shows up at vintage clothing shops, was a big local clothing store at the time. It leased the entire second floor and was in operation for over twenty years. Attorney General James M. Ashton also had an office in the building. A would-be tragedy turned into a farce when the well-known attorney was attacked. On January 23, 1931, fifty-year-old Andrew Marr, an angry coal miner, walked into the general's office and thrust a piece of paper in the attorney's hand.

"Sign this or there will be trouble," he said.

The general started talking to Marr while at the same time backing him out of the office. But Marr caught on and whipped a pistol out of his pocket. The seventy-two-year-old general grabbed the man's wrist, and the two began scuffling—fighting for possession of the gun. A second attorney, William R. Lee, heard the racket, rushed in and made a flying leap at Marr. He landed on the man's back, they both went down and then Marr flung Lee under a table. Stenographer Lucile Davenport, who also heard the fight, called the police. As she hung up, someone fired two shots. She rushed in, stepped between Marr and the general and was roughly pushed away by Marr. She then grabbed him by the wrist and ordered him to give her the gun. To everyone's amazement, he did. After that, she frisked him for more weapons and told him to sit down. When the police arrived, he was cowering in a chair while she kept his own gun trained on him. Just before officers led Marr away, he said goodbye and shook hands with the general. At the police station, the story came out.

Marr claimed that General Ashton owed him $25,000. The previous October, Marr had sued the Carbon Hill and Oil Company for $20,000. During testimony in federal court, it was proved that a contract giving Marr $25,000 if he "secured the election" of Martin Flyzik as president of the mine workers' union in 1913 was bogus. General Ashton was both a witness and council for the coal company. Marr said he never really meant to kill General Ashton, but he was held in jail for attempted murder anyway.

Two years after the shooting, KVI radio moved into the Rust Building. KVI had been on the air as a part-time station, broadcasting out of a small facility and sharing time with KMO. However, Tacoma residents demanded a full-time station. More than twenty thousand letters poured into the Federal Radio Commission, which granted KVI that status.

The new status required a bigger studio.

"We want a station second to none," E.M. Doernbecher, president of the Puget Sound Broadcasting Company, said.

The company rented three thousand square feet of space on the building's southwest side and finished the rooms with western knotty cedar, weathered oak and hammered iron chandeliers. A large studio made of Weyerhaeuser Nu-Wood was actually a room within a room. It included balsam curtains to ensure soundproofing.

These were not good years for the Rust Building, however, and they should have been because even before completion the building was blessed with a baptism.

On August 7, 1920, Earl L. Powell took his baby and began climbing up an unsteady, swaying series of ladders, after which he walked carefully over isolated six-inch girders, two-by-fours and sagging planks to the tenth floor, all the while dodging rivets and flying board ends. Waiting for him, on temporary flooring, were C.V. Crumley, Mr. Powell's boss; Charles Perryman Gaumond, a Seattle cameraman; M.D. Boland, a photographer; a *Tacoma Daily Ledger* reporter; and fifty structural steelworkers who acted as godfathers to the baby, little Marjorie. Then, Mason Methodist Church's Reverend Joseph O. Marlatt, holding a bowl of water, and R. Crawford, a structural worker who held Marjorie during the ceremony, mounted a girder at rest on the platform, and with men grasping the derrick chains, the girder was hoisted fifteen feet from the tenth story and swung out over Eleventh Street. While men shouted, boards crashed, riveters riveted and street traffic filled the air, Marjorie crowed with delight as she was anointed. The girder was then lowered back to the tenth floor, where all the godfathers gathered to shake the baby's hand. There's no word on where Mrs. Powell was during all this.

The girder to God didn't protect the Rust Building. William Rust died in 1928. A year later, Townsend and Company Investment Bankers leased the building and changed the name. Two years later, the company went bankrupt. The court gave the building to W.R. Rust Investment Company, and the Rust name was reinstated. Arthur Rust, William's son, said how pleased the Rust estate was.

On January 1, 1937, G-men took up headquarters there during the Charles Mattson kidnapping. In September 1942, a man fell down the elevator shaft. During the Red Scare of the 1950s, the Rust Building had an air raid shelter. The building was remodeled in 1985 and reopened in 1986 with a new look. Pink marble, gargoyles, large plants and artwork salvaged from the top were relocated to the lobby for people to enjoy.

DRINK TO ME ONLY WITH THINE EYES, BUT THE BREWERIES WILL OBJECT

One thing that was true of every frontier town was that they were populated by thirsty, hardworking men who wanted beer. And saloons were among the first buildings to go up. Until the advent of local breweries, beer was shipped in from larger cities, but as soon as a brew master arrived, he usually started to make his own. And for a small, developing frontier town, Tacoma had quite a few breweries.

Ignatz Fuerst established the New Tacoma Brewery at 2331 Fawcett Avenue in 1884. There isn't any information about it other than that, according to

Here's to you!

the history of the Milwaukee Brewing Company, a man named Diedrich Stegmann established a brewery the same year at the same site. He ran it as a sole proprietorship until 1886 and then took on a partner, Henry Lusthoff. The two formed a new company, the United States Brewing & Ice Company. Their Fawcett Street address also included 2330 Jefferson Avenue.

Four years later, two other men, Zacharias Zimmerman and George Harrel, a wealthy brewer who already owned the United States Brewing Company of Portland, entered Tacoma's beer market. They got in as a result of reorganizing the Stegmann and Lusthoff brewery. The new stock company, with Stegmann as president and a man named Mathies Karasek as secretary/treasurer, lasted three years. In 1891, local liquor dealers Samuel S. Loeb and Albert Weinberg, along with various other businessmen primarily from the Jewish community, bought the United States Brewery and renamed it the Milwaukee Brewing Company.

Soon after the reorganization, a *Tacoma Daily Ledger* article announced that the plant was being enlarged. The new facility consisted of four buildings. The office building, part of which was the superintendent's residence, was 25 by 80 feet and two and a half stories high. The four-story storehouse, which measured 120 by 40 feet, included the brewery proper. Beer was brewed in a fifty-barrel kettle, and the kettle could be used twice a day, though at that time Milwaukee was turning out only fifty barrels daily. A refrigeration system cooled fifty barrels an hour. And a fifty-horsepower boiler and engine kept it all running. The brewery did its own hauling, so it housed fifteen horses in a two-story, on-site stable measuring 30 by 44 feet.

One of the changes under consideration at the time of the enlargement was adding a malt house to store germinated grain, which beer brewing requires. Most Puget Sound breweries imported everything from San Francisco; however, Milwaukee used Puyallup Valley hops and kept 120 bales on hand.

Thanks to the enlargement and improvements, the company had a daily capability of 125 barrels. A year-end recap of the business stated that Milwaukee had increased its annual output to sixty thousand barrels valued at $200,000, employed twenty-three men and had a payroll of $2,250.

Two years after establishing the company, the partners incorporated the business and issued 350 shares of stock. Misters Loeb and Weinberg were trustees, and a man named Kasper Hoffmeir was the brew master. An Interstate Fair held on October 7, 1894, featured a German-American Day. According to the newspaper, members of the German-American community had been indefatigable in their efforts to put the Milwaukee Brewing Company in the front line of West Coast brewery houses.

Of course, Milwaukee wasn't the only brewery in Tacoma. The Donau Brewing Company opened in 1888 at 1001–23 East Twenty-sixth Street; the Old Tacoma Brewery opened in 1889 at the rear portion of a lot at 2118–22 North Thirtieth Street. The next big one was Puget Sound Brewery (PSB) at 2501–15 Jefferson, although the address is now considered to be 2500 South Holgate.

PSB, owned by Anton Huth and John Scholl, started in a four-story building measuring eighty by eighty feet but quickly added a forty- by forty-foot wing. It had a steam-heated beer boiler with a capacity of 4,300 gallons and a mashing machine that held 6,500 barrels and produced 260 barrels a day under the brand names Walhalla and Der Goetten Trank. The owners incorporated in 1891 with Scholl as president, but three years later Mr. Huth bought him out. Mr. Scholl went to Chico, California, and bought a brewery there, and Mr. Huth ran Puget Sound Brewing until 1897. He then took on a partner named William Virges, and the two made plans to take over the local competition. PSB merged with Milwaukee Brewery, creating a new company called Pacific Brewing & Malting Company, and Milwaukee Brewery officially closed in 1899. The new company undertook major expansion projects, one of which was to start Washington Brewing Co. in Everett. Another was to aid in the startup of a second brewery in Tacoma, the Columbia Brewing Company.

In 1900, Emil Kliese, a German-born brew master, came to Tacoma. When he couldn't find work as a brew master, he decided to start his

Columbia Brewing label. *Courtesy of BreweryGems.com.*

own brewery. Kliese and a man named Willian Kiltz filed articles of incorporation on February 8, 1900. Pacific Brewing and Malting was a major shareholder. Work on Columbia Brewing began in 1900 at 2120–32 South C (Broadway). It was in a five-story wooden building built over an artesian well. Columbia's output was fifty barrels a day under several brands: Columbia, Golden Drops, Golden foam and Old Pilsner. In 1912, it added Alt Heidelberg.

Pacific Brewing completed its expansion in 1905, but shareholders weren't happy. They felt that the merger deals were underwriting expansions, and they wanted larger dividend payments. Samuel Loeb brought a lawsuit requesting that Pacific Brewing sell its interests in the Everett Company and in Columbia. The sale left Loeb in a very good financial position—until Washington went dry.

Prohibition came to Washington State in 1916, several years before the Volstead Act. Pacific Brewing began making cocoanut butter and high-grade soaps. Columbia became Columbia Bottling Company and made soft drinks such as Birch Beer, Chocolate Soldier, Blue Jay and Green River. In 1919, the company introduced a near beer called Colo and, in 1925, a new soft drink called Orange Kist.

Heidelberg bought Columbia Brewery in 1949 and, four years later, changed its name to Heidelberg Brewing Company. The company dropped the "alt" from the name of what became its flagship beer. Then, in 1953, Carling Brewing Company of Canada bought Heidelberg.

The history of Tacoma's first breweries is complicated. The same men were buying, selling and merging both here and with breweries in Seattle.

After repeal of the Volstead Act, even more breweries came along. Northwest Brewing Co. relocated to 105–07 East Thirty-sixth Street in 1931. Independent Breweries, Inc., followed in 1934 at 5624 McKinley Avenue. In 1950, Port Orchard's Silver Springs Brewery also relocated to East Twenty-sixth. And these are just the legal breweries. Illegal liquor is a story all its own.

A ROOF WITH A ZOO: THE WASHINGTON BUILDING

Until a Tacoma medical laboratory decided a roof was a terrible thing to waste, the Washington Building had a fairly humdrum existence. It began on July 27, 1919, when the *Tacoma Daily Ledger* announced that Tacoma was getting a new fifteen-story building to be called the Scandinavian Bank Building. However, from then until the following January, the papers had very little information. On January 4, 1920, readers were told that it would be sixteen not fifteen stories, would replace an existing bank building at Eleventh Street and Pacific Avenue and would be second to none to on the Pacific coast. Depositors were advised that the existing bank's business would be moved to Thirteenth and Pacific. The architect, who was interested in using as much Tacoma labor as possible, asked all the local contractors to put in their bids.

By the end of February, many individual contracts had been issued: Tacoma's Ben Olson Company would handle all the plumbing and heating; the Tacoma Mill Work Supply Company would do all the interior finishing, which included mahogany wainscoting and sash and door work; Hunt and Mottet, a business that is still around, would provide the hardware; Far West Clay was responsible for all the tile; and a Spokane company, Washington Brick and Terra Cotta, would provide terra cotta for the walls. Washington Brick was the only company in the state that could furnish the necessary materials in the specified time. Brick from the old building had been salvaged for reuse; the bank floor was going to be granite. Various aspects of the construction were job by job because apparently Tacoma contractors had failed to submit complete bids. And since a Seattle man named Nick Georig was already doing excavation work across the street for the new Rust Building, he was given the excavation contract. Construction continued throughout the rest of the year. More contracts were issued. Standard Oil leased the entire tenth floor, steel shipped from East Coast mills arrived and the beams attracted all kinds of attention, not all of it good.

Many years after the bank was complete, a Swedish man named Anders Johansson was interviewed as part of Pacific Lutheran University's oral history project. He said that in the 1920s he was the caretaker at a Covenant Bay beach camp, earning thirty-five cents an hour. The camp director, a Norwegian named Wendels, told Mr. Johansson that the Americans wanted the Scandinavians to invest their money in the Bank of California and other Tacoma banks because the Scandinavians were considered industrious and prosperous, and the men wanted the Scandinavian-American Bank out of the way. The bank did go away, but not because of the investment practices of men such as Mr. Johansson.

On the morning of January 14, 1921, there was a sort of a milk run on the bank. However, thanks to rumors that had been swirling around town, many people who had been issued checks from the bank found that some local stores refused to honor them, and contrary to its custom, the bank didn't remain open to cash pay checks. The following evening, state bank commissioner Claude P. Hay closed it with a brief but devastating statement.

In 1917, the bank's president, J.S. Chilberg, lobbied for creating the Washington Bank Depositor's Guarantee Fund. Mr. Hay issued a statement saying that while every other bank in Tacoma was a member of the Federal Reserve System and the state's Association of Banks, which guaranteed bank deposits, the Scandinavian-American Bank was not. Hay said that though the bank had repeatedly claimed the building had been financed by outside capital, it wasn't true. Approximately $1,200,000 of the depositors' funds had been used. The twelve thousand depositors could expect to possibly be repaid 75 percent.

On January 15, 1921, Chilberg surrendered himself to answer five indictments issued in King County. Four of the charges were for making excessive loans to himself, and the fifth was that he lent a large sum of money to one of the bank's directors without the authority of the board of directors. According to an article on Historylink.org, Chilberg's case was principally a problem of his stewardship of the bank. Chilberg had been one of the most prominent men in the Pacific Northwest, especially in Seattle, and a King County Grand Jury found him not guilty.

The collapse left many depositors holding the proverbial bag—in this case, an empty one. Putting a human spin on the issue, one report stated that most of the depositors who lost their savings were from the "humbler walks of life."

Anything You Can Do, Tacoma Can Do Better

In the meantime, the bank's steel skeleton was erected to its full height, and the brickwork was completed to the twelfth floor. It stayed that way for several years.

On April 28, 1925, a young man named Wolstiuholme (no first name given in the paper) snuck up the back stairs of the uncompleted building, went to the northwest cornice, took off his jacket and stood on his head. Seventeen stories below, people watching from the street were thrilled. A police detective and the foreman took a lift to the roof and saw the boy with his feet pointing skyward. However, they didn't know how to approach him without "causing a serious accident." After Wolstiuholme was right side up, he said he'd been doing stunts such as this one since he could walk, and he was just looking for some excitement. The detective explained that such displays required a license and took the young man to jail. He was interviewed, found to be sincere and given a job working on the building.

Construction was finally done, and the building opened for business on June 29, 1925. Its major tenant, Brotherhood Bank, opened on July 2. On July 5, there was a rooftop party. At 4:30 p.m., a delegation of California realtors arrived at the Union Depot and was met by twenty men, sixteen women and a fourteen-member glee club in a caravan of cars supplied by Tacoma realtors. The California delegation was driven across the Eleventh

The Washington Building's zoo. *Lenard Eccles, artist.*

Street Bridge for a tour of the waterfront and Tacoma's industrial section and then back to town for a reception on the roof. After the cocktail hour, they were driven through the Stadium residential district and on to Point Defiance for a picnic supper.

From then on, life at the Washington Building was fairly quiet until the aforementioned biological laboratory decided to establish a scientific zoo on the roof. It brought in mice, guinea pigs, rats developed by the Wistar Institute of Anatomy and Flemish giant rabbits. According to the paper, the rabbits were important in "criminal experiments and medico-legal work where the authorities sought to determine whether bloodstains were those of humans or animals." Scientists did this by inoculating a rabbit with human blood and, after a certain period of time, testing the chemical reaction of the rabbit's blood on the stains discovered at a crime scene. Also, "the experiment had to be carried on indefinitely by the inoculation of the rabbit with the blood of other animals if it is desired to determine the exact nature of the bloodstains." The guinea pigs were used for various diseases to determine a diagnosis in cases where the microscope was unable to detect disease. The mice were valuable in determining the four different types of pneumonia, and the rats were used for diet tests and food research. The rats had a slightly better life in that they were allowed to breed.

After the '20s, nothing particularly unusual happened at the Washington Building. Businesses came and went; the Tacoma Club leased quarters in 1937 and stayed until 1991. And a little seven-bed hospital operated there (the pun's intentional). It was the predecessor of Allenmore Hospital.

DANCING WITH THE STARS, OR AT LEAST UNDER THEM: THE WINTHROP HOTEL

At nearly ninety years old, the Winthrop Hotel is no longer the shining star of Tacoma it once was. Over the years, since its completion in 1925, the hotel has been remodeled and its purpose reinvented several times, but now it's just a venerable old building with a great history and questionable future.

The drive to build a top tourist hotel in Tacoma began on May 14, 1922, with the formation of a group of citizens who called themselves the Flying Squadron. They went from business to business, soliciting investors, and eventually 2,300 people chipped in to form what was initially called the Citizens Hotel Corporation. From then until it opened on May 15, 1925, local newspapers covered every aspect of the hotel's construction.

The articles began with an announcement on March 13, 1923, that the Daniel M. Linnard Company had obtained a hotel lease on the building. Mr. Linnard was a well-known hotel tycoon whose other hotel interests were mainly in California. The 1920s were the "Age of Great Hotel Resorts," and he was prominent in a number of ventures.

After the deal with Linnard closed, the corporation had a year in which to build the hotel. A call for bids went out on April 25, 1923. A contract was let on May 11. On May 27, the *Tacoma Daily Ledger* printed a sketch of the interior plans, and in July, it announced a contest to give the hotel a name that was better than Citizens Hotel. George Dickson, owner of Dickson Brothers clothing company, won the contest when he suggested Winthrop in honor of explorer and writer Theodore Winthrop.

Two hundred construction workers began work on the Winthrop in December. The result was a ten-story building with addresses on two different streets: 761–83 Broadway and 762–86 Commerce. From the Commerce Street entrance, a half flight of stairs led to the mezzanine. Another half flight ended at the ballroom, and a quarter flight of steps went down to the lobby. Guests' bedrooms were on eight floors. Each had a private shower or bath. Gregory Furniture Company of Tacoma made the rooms' beds, desks, tables and wooden chairs using American walnut. Carman Manufacturing, also of Tacoma, provided the mattresses. The Immanuel

The Winthrop Hotel, circa 1935.

Presbyterian Church of Tacoma donated Bibles. In addition, each room had a telephone, but calls had to be connected through the private branch exchange switchboard located on the roof near the garden. Guest floors were accessed by five elevators. Each landing had its own little lobby.

The Broadway entrance opened onto a combination lobby and dining room that measured 40 by 120 feet. Five tall Italian-style floor lamps provided light. Furnishings included small hexagonal tables with Rookwood pottery bowls on them and small lamps of blue Chinese porcelain with gold-fringed shades of Chinese embroidered crepe.

A main feature at the Winthrop was its 38- by 120-foot Crystal Ballroom. The ballroom had vaulted ceilings with four six-hundred-pound, Austrian-cut crystal chandeliers and twenty six-candle wall brackets draped with crystals. Cream-colored enamel walls were accented with dark wainscoting. There was old-rose relief work highlighted with gold and plenty of mirrors. Those who wanted to watch the dancing could do so from a small balcony.

The Winthrop's top floor had a rooftop garden dining room painted burnt orange and black. Art glass in the ceiling hid the lights. Guests entered a foyer with a terra cotta marble floor and then walked under a vaulted archway decorated with stars and moons. Tacoma's Washington Parlor Company provided specially designed reed dining room furniture. For intimate dinners, the hotel had two small dining rooms: one blue and one rose and gold. A sliding door separated them. They were finished in mahogany and had columns of inlaid panel relief work. Above the columns' heads were shields and coats of arms. All the public parts of the building were marble with ornamental iron balustrades. The final construction cost was $2,500,000.

A few weeks prior to the grand opening, the Linnard hotel organization sent a pastry chef to train the kitchen staff in the fine art of cakes, pies, bread and rolls. The chef allowed the paper to print six of his recipes and challenged Tacoma homemakers to give them a try. His waffles called for brandy in dough that had to rise three hours before it was baked, not fried. No one is on record as having accepted the challenge.

On May 15, the general public was allowed in to have a look. The grand opening was the next day. People came from all over Washington, Oregon, California and British Columbia. However, though 3,000 were expected, only 1,700 showed up—the women in evening gowns and the men in tuxedos. It was the style, in those days, to send telegrams on such occasions. Dozens arrived, coming from New York, Pittsburgh, Chicago, Detroit, Philadelphia and Washington, D.C. Flowers filled the rooms where people dined and danced. The *Tacoma Sunday Daily Ledger* called the meal a "culinary triumph of French cuisine." Thereafter, having tea at the Winthrop became *de rigueur.*

Eight days after the grand opening, KBG radio station began broadcasting from the Winthrop. Then a thirty-five-foot arrow pointing toward the airport was put on the roof to help out low-flying planes.

One of the Winthrop's most exciting events was a thirty-one-hour flagpole dance put on by entertainers Betty and Benny Fox, a circus act that was advertised as a brother-and-sister circus, though they are now known to have been husband and wife.

They came to town in the middle of the June 1934 and began practicing for the event, sometimes on a little platform sixty feet above ground and sometimes on the roof's cornices. While they cavorted, a small dancing platform—a circle of wood about twenty-four inches across—was attached to the top of the roof's flagpole. People used binoculars or spyglasses to watch them. When Benny picked Betty up, one of the papers made a subtle remark about modesty. The paper also sent up a handwriting expert to get some writing samples for examination. Benny was wearing white overalls over his regular clothes. He felt his pockets and said he forgot to include pen and paper.

When asked what they would do when they came down, Betty said they might go dancing. It all made for a good story to help with the general anxiety of the Depression.

Try as it might, though, the Winthrop never made any money. Its only era of prosperity was World War II. At first, stockholders received a few cents in dividend payments, but the original investors never did get their money back.

As of this writing, the Grand Dame is low-income housing, but the Crystal Ballroom is exactly as it was in 1948 when actor Peter Lorre was there signing autographs.

Part III

Civilized Living

THE HOTEL HESPERIDES: GRACIOUS LIVING AT TITLOW LODGE

At the beginning of the twentieth century, Titlow Lodge was Tacoma's smaller-in-every-way answer to Michigan's Grand Hotel on Mackinac Island. While Titlow Lodge was on two hundred acres, the Mackinac resort covered 3.8 square miles. While Titlow Lodge had a sizeable porch, the Grand Hotel's porch was once the longest in the world. But hey, they were both on water—the Grand Hotel on Mackinac Island in Lake Heron and the Hotel Hesperides on a stretch of Puget Sound at the bottom of Sixth Avenue.

Today, little remains of the lodge Aaron Titlow called Hesperides in honor of his daughters and which calls for knowledge of Greek mythology. The Hesperides were nymphs who attended a blissful garden.

Before white men came along, the Puyallup and Nisqually Indians called the site Tranquil Bay and often camped there. However, the land eventually became part of William B. Wilton's donation land claim. In 1903, Mr. Wilton sold the property to Ohio-born Aaron Titlow and his business partner, state fish commissioner A.C. Little. Right away, Mr. Titlow began promoting an extension to and the paving of Sixth Avenue down as far as his property. Seven years later, the Northern Pacific Railroad paid the two men $55,000 for a right of way, a move that eventually came back to bite Mr. Titlow.

Thanks to advertising, Tacoma was in the midst of a tourism boom, and Pierce County prosecuting attorney Aaron Titlow was well aware of this. In 1911, he used the majority of his railroad money to begin the process of building a luxury hotel/resort.

However, right from the start, when he began dredging the lagoon, his actions got Mr. Titlow mixed up in a lawsuit over land use. The issues involved were twofold: Tacoma's right to condemn and appropriate a right of way over certain land both in and outside city limits and the need for the state legislature to locate and establish harbor lines in the navigable waters of all the state's harbors, bays and inlets. Once these issues were resolved—oddly enough in Mr. Titlow's favor because courts weren't so much into all that eminent domain stuff the way they are now—he built a house; planted orchards and vegetable gardens; brought in horses, pigs and a herd of pure-blood Jersey cows; and started a dairy. Finally, after these preliminaries were done, he started building his resort hotel.

The Golden Age of Resorts was all about going someplace where people dressed for dinner and strolled afterward on open, covered verandas with pleasant views while listening to an orchestra playing somewhere in the background. And that was exactly the place and ambiance that Mr. Titlow created.

Frederick Heath, who had already designed Stadium and Lincoln High Schools, Central School and the Knights of Pythias Temple, among many other buildings in Tacoma, was the architect. What he came up with was a three-and-a-half-story Swiss chalet that faced west toward the water where, all day long, steamships, tugboats, rowboats and three- and four-masted ships passed by, headed for Tacoma or for Olympia and Shelton. The cedar and pine lodge had thirty two-room suites, each with a private bath and usually a private balcony. Hot and cold fresh and salt water was piped to each suite. A concrete basement had a large fireplace, billiard room and barbershop. The housekeeper and servants' quarters were on the top floor, where the guests' luggage was stored. In the dining room, twenty-two Tiffany lanterns illuminated tables set with linen, china and silver. Columns of Douglas fir supported beamed ceilings, and at one end of the room was another large fireplace. In fact, the resort had a number of fireplaces.

The Titlow farm had an ostrich farm where the nine-foot birds ran around squawking. As a result, the breakfast menu offered ostrich eggs. A typical dinner was chicken and dumplings, fresh vegetables and salads, pie made from different kinds of berries and peach butter. The original Titlow farm provided all the food.

Civilized Living

Veranda of the Hotel Hesperides. *Courtesy of Robin Paterson.*

The custom, in those days, was for the ladies to withdraw after dinner. At the lodge, they had a choice of adjourning to a ladies' parlor or a covered pergola across the back with floors of Moravian blue tiles. Meanwhile, their husbands discussed business, smoked cigars and drank brandy—or they would have had a brandy except for one thing: the ladies of half a dozen neighborhood churches joined together to have the lodge's liquor license denied.

During long, lazy summer days, guests dug clams, hunted for crabs and went beachcombing or fishing. Some hiked in nearby groves of giant cedar, fir and maple trees. Others played tennis on the lodge's courts, took their children to the wading pool or swam in the lagoon. Mr. Titlow had a small dam, which included sea locks, constructed. The locks held the lagoon's water at a stationary level a few feet below high tide, and the incoming and outgoing tides changed the water every twelve hours. There were also campsites if people wanted to come and put up tents on the grounds. And in the 1920s, guests could walk across the street to the Weaver Studios and see how a movie was made.

The hotel had its own dock and owned a glass-bottomed boat and two other boats, the *Folly* and the *Lady of the Lake*, which were used to transport guests to Day Island, Fox Island, Wollochet Bay and other nearby islands and inlets.

Hotel Hesperides.

Guests arrived by both boat and car and came from as far away as New Jersey. Chauffeurs stayed in a two-story building separate from the resort. Their bedrooms and baths were upstairs; downstairs was for the limousines. That building was eventually moved near the lagoon and became a bathhouse.

And then in the end, there was the shooting oneself in the foot thing, figuratively speaking. First, Mr. Titlow never wanted to actually run the place himself, and the various majordomos he hired weren't very good at it. And second, in 1913, the Northern Pacific Railroad built a railroad line on the land he'd sold to it, separating the resort from the beach. It was a case of the railroad giveth and the railroad taketh away, and the clickety-clack of trains racing by was no one's idea of a high-end resort asset.

Times changed. In the off-season, young bachelors made the Hesperides their home. When World War I came along, the army housed officers and their families in the resort. After the war, high-style beach resort vacations faded in popularity. The lodge quit making a profit, and Mr. Titlow sold out. In 1928, the Metropolitan Park District bought the land, concessionaires ran the hotel and people came merely to swim in the lagoon. During the Depression, a WPA project was launched to enlarge the park facilities. Workers cleared away great portions of underbrush and fallen timber, created roads and trails and built a boathouse, restrooms and community shelters. A custodian moved into the front part of the hotel, and the top floors were taken off, leaving one and a half stories. The Park Department put on a new roof, remodeled the kitchen, added new restrooms and either added or replaced parts of the floor with refinished oak. The dining room became a public meeting room. Some of the old interior support beams were crooked—one park district employee said they twisted like a snake— and had to be replaced. In 1955, the old swimming lagoon was retired, and an Olympic-sized swimming pool was put in. The cost to upgrade the structure alone was $187,000. There's no word on whether the sale of those Tiffany lanterns paid for anything.

THE ICEMAN COMETH

A prevailing can-do attitude in the 1880s was widespread in Tacoma. So when businessmen organized a company to build a sixty-mile chute from Mount Rainier's Nisqually glacier to town, the idea seemed perfectly feasible. Residents needed the mountain's ice, so why not cut blocks and slide them down a chute? Well, no one ever said every idea was a good one.

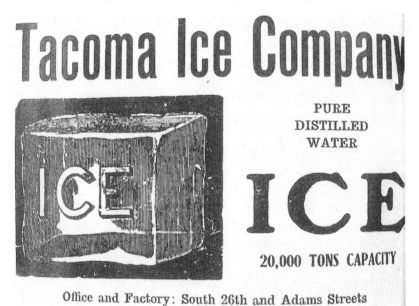

Advertisement for Tacoma Ice.

As soon as ice did become available in Tacoma, Mrs. Alice Blackwell built an icebox. She selected two stout wooden boxes of different sizes so that one would fit inside the other with about a two-inch space on all sides; she then packed the space with sawdust. She removed the lid of the inner box and reattached it with hinges, put a piece of ice in the bottom of the box and a sheet of wood over the ice and used the box to keep butter, milk and eggs cold. As the ice melted, the water soaked through the sawdust and ran out through a hole. She found the instructions in the June 1875 issue of the *American Agriculturist*.

Tacoma got ice in 1887 when the Tacoma Ice and Storage Company built a facility on Holgate Street. The company owned twelve horses and employed fourteen men who made deliveries by wagon. The deliverymen wore leather aprons that hung down their backs and used pronged clamps to grip the blocks they carried over their shoulders. In addition to town, Tacoma Ice delivered to cities along the railroad lines in the southern part of the state and eastern Washington. People such as Mrs. Blackwell subscribed to ice delivery. Sometimes subscribers put in special orders for things such as flowers, bottles of wine, fish or game to be frozen in a block.

In the United States, the ice business started early in the nineteenth century when a man named William Tudor visited the Caribbean and decided he could create a business shipping ice there. In 1806, he bought the brig *Favorite* to carry frozen pond water from Boston to Martinique and, at the same time, sent his brother, Frederick, and cousin James to various Caribbean governments to secure contracts for Tudor ice. By 1810, William's profits totaled $9,000, but he was only able to keep $1,000 because of what he called the "villainous conduct of his ice agent." Gradually, William's debits exceeded his income, and he spent parts of 1812 and 1813 in debtor's prison. In 1815, he borrowed $2,100; had an icehouse built in Havana, Cuba; bought ice; and set sail with the sheriff, as he said, "pursuing him right to the wharf."

His subsequent trips were so successful that William decided to experiment by exporting tropical fruits from Cuba to the United States preserved in fifteen tons of ice and three tons of hay. Once again, he ended up in debt. Nevertheless, William soldiered on, experimenting with sawdust, wood shavings and rice chaff as insulations and learning to have the ice cut and packed like masonry blocks. He built icehouses on various tropical islands and created a demand for ice drinks. William was doing well, but cutting the blocks correctly was difficult and expensive—until a man named Nathaniel Jarvis Wyeth harnessed horses to a metal blade to cut ice in blocks of twenty-five, fifty and one hundred pounds. Wyeth's ice plow made mass production a reality and allowed William to more than triple his production.

In 1833, Boston-based merchant Samuel Austin proposed a partnership for selling ice to India, some sixteen thousand miles and four months away from Massachusetts. On May 12, 1833, the brig *Tuscany* sailed from Boston for Calcutta, carrying 180 tons of ice in its hold. When the ship approached the Ganges in September 1833, many believed the delivery was an elaborate joke, but the *Tuscany* still had 100 tons of ice on arrival. Over the next twenty years, Calcutta became William's most lucrative destination, yielding an estimated $220,000 in profits.

In the early 1830s, William also began to speculate in coffee futures with his ice business as collateral. Initially, coffee prices did rise, and he made millions of dollars, but in 1834, he fell more than a quarter million dollars in debt, forcing him to refocus on the ice trade. By then, the ice business had expanded from New York up through Maine. Newly constructed railroad lines sped up the process of transporting ice and made it more efficient. By the 1840s, ice was being shipped all over the world, and although William Tudor was now just a small part of the trade, his profits allowed him to pay off his debts and live a very comfortable life.

Meanwhile, in 1861, an icebox was developed. It was very much like Mrs. Blackwell's, except that manufactured iceboxes were lined with lead or zinc and had shelves and compartments. And in Tacoma, as elsewhere, trucks gradually replaced horse-drawn delivery wagons. Tacoma Ice built a new five-story brick cold-storage building in 1923.

When refrigerators came along, stockholders wanted a more aggressive management team. John and Pat Reisinger bought the company and began packaging a new product called party ice. They still packaged ice blocks but also made and sold ten-pound blocks of ice and snow, crushed ice in large and small bags and dry ice.

Thirty-nine years later, the *News Tribune* declared that the ice age here was officially over. The Olsen family of Parkland finally decided to get rid of their icebox. Mr. Olsen said keeping it around was too much of a luxury. During the summer months, the Olsens used five to six hundred pounds of ice, and that was okay when it was one and a half cents a pound. However, in August, their ice bill had been eighteen dollars, so they felt forced to change to a refrigerator. The Olsens were not a family who liked change. For years they had lived on a house on the PLU campus. When the college decided to enlarge, rather than move to a new house, they moved the house to a new location.

At the time the Olsens made the big change, Tacoma Ice still had five men delivering ice, mostly to businesses. A fire destroyed part of the building on March 5, 1979, and the ice-making portion was rebuilt in a separate structure.

These days, the occupation of ice delivery lives on mainly in Amish communities.

WAITRESS! THERE'S A FLY IN MY FOOD! ESTHER ALLSTRUM AND THE CLEAN FOODS ACTS

In one restaurant in Seattle a sewer overflows and floods the floor and people are compelled to eat food prepared in such places.
—Delegate Alice Lord addressing the State Federation of Labor

Service with a smile.

Alice Lord, who made her statement on January 11, 1908, went on to say that cooks and waitresses were often expected to change their clothes in the bathrooms, many of which were located in the kitchen. Clearly, reforms were called for, and that's where Esther Allstrum came in. For three years, she was Tacoma's food inspector.

Miss Allstum was born in Minnesota to Louis and Eva Allstrum, who had come to the States from Stockholm, Sweden. She went to school in Minnesota, but after that reports differ. She either learned the printing trade in Minnesota and then came to Tacoma or she came to Tacoma and learned the printing trade here. Either way, she found work as an apprentice press feeder and moved on to typesetting, ruling and binding. Ruling means she drew lines on blank paper, and though lined paper dates to the early nineteenth century, it had yet to become common. The books Miss Allstrum was ruling and binding were used by the first Alaska federal court, over which Judge James Wickersham presided. There were eighty of these books in all. She managed both the mechanical aspects of the job and then the business side, after which she became a partner in the firm. Miss Allstrum had what was normally considered to be a good-paying *man's* job, and the men in the office weren't shy about making her life there difficult any time they could.

The 1891 *Tacoma City Directory* lists her as working for Washington Book Bindery. Two years later, she was associated with the Western Blank Book Company. From there, she went to work for Waller Printing Company. In 1909, Miss Allstrum went into the printing business for herself, opening the Allstrum Printing Company at 729 Commerce. Because of her broad background, she was able to show a profit almost immediately. In fact, her printing business became one of the most comprehensive in the state.

In 1911, she hired her brother, David, who for the previous fourteen years had been an employee of the Carstens Packing Company, where he worked his way up to company treasure. This move may have been necessary because the previous year Mayor Angelo Fawcett had made Miss Allstrum Tacoma's city food inspector, replacing Mrs. Mary Macready. According to reports, Mayor Fawcett appointed Miss Allstrum to the post because Mrs. Macready had been excessively competent, and he was hoping Miss Allstrum would be too busy with her printing business or, as he put it, with her "money-making affairs" to bother with inspecting food.

"I've lived a long time without having my food inspected," he said, "and I've never been poisoned yet." Unfortunately for the mayor, Miss Allstrum was equally vigorous in pursuing dishonest and lackadaisical market operators.

At the time, Tacoma had one thousand food dealers, of whom only two hundred had their proper licenses. So she started by insisting that all the city's food dealers take out a one-dollar license. She made lists of the food regulations and asked grocers and butchers to frame and post the food ordinances on their premises. Naturally, there was sizeable opposition, and the merchants started asking her how far she was prepared to enforce the rules. "All the way to the Supreme Court," she told them. It was tough going, though, because the market owners just didn't want to comply. When that happened, Miss Allstrum would sometimes go to the newspapers. Once, she found that spoiled clams were being used to make clam nectar. She could

The danger of bad food.

have just gotten the proof and worked through conventional methods to stop their sale. Instead, because she wanted the sales to stop immediately, she gave the facts to a reporter. After the paper got involved, clam nectar became a very unpopular drink in Tacoma.

Another time, she poured kerosene over a box of food scraps that a dealer claimed was bologna, and at yet another market, when the shopkeeper had been warned to move his sidewalk display inside the sidewalk line and refused, she sawed the legs off his table.

In those days, Tacoma had a public market on South D Street, and she demanded that the market make improvements. One was the construction of uniform stalls or stands for every dealer who rented space. Contractors built thirty-four new stalls, which were eleven feet, four inches long and five feet high at one end and two feet high at the other. The result was a sloping stand eight feet deep for its full length. The entire stand was raised above the street level more than eighteen inches, permitting merchants to wash out any refuse that might gather underneath. The new stalls made the whole market easier to clean. Another improvement came when she arranged for additional tanks and pipes needed to supply greater amounts of water for said cleaning. Since the city paid for all this, it naturally charged fees. Interestingly enough, in spite of the fees, there was an increased demand for the new stalls.

Nationally, magazines began picking up her success story and named her "the woman who has made Tacoma famous for its model food ordinance." Inquiries came in from all over. Her track record caused Seattle, Spokane and Yakima to appoint female food inspectors.

Miss Allstrum was making major headways in cleaning up Tacoma's food when one of the newspapers published an account claiming that in order to keep his office, Mayor Fawcett had promised to appoint a new inspector, one with lax standards. Once this got out, the dealers ignored Miss Allstrum's orders, and the authorities ignored her appeals for help. Finally, she resigned. In a letter to the newspapers, she said, "The situation has become intolerable, and for my self-respect I cannot [any] longer hold this office and be a party to the betrayal of the pure-food law."

As it turned out, Mayor Fawcett didn't appoint a new food inspector, and the office remained vacant until he was out of office and William Seymour was elected. The public demanded that Miss Allstrum be reappointed, but she said the strain of the job was too great, and besides she had her own business to run. However, when the mayor appealed to her "ardent suffrage beliefs," she changed her mind and worked for him until his administration ended.

In addition to her job as food inspector, Miss Allstrum was a charter member of the YWCA and belonged to the United States Typothetae [*sic*] of America, which later became the Printing Industries of America. She was a member of the Woman's Club of Tacoma, was state treasurer of the National Council of Women Voters, was a member of the Republican county executive committee and was the only female member of the Employers' Association of the State of Washington.

Miss Allstrum bought a house at 644 Trafton in 1906 and lived in it until her death in 1917. The house is still there.

THE EYE OF THE LAW FALLS ON WOMEN

One day in the last quarter of the nineteenth century, a woman named Bethena Owens Adair—wife, mother, domestic, teacher, milliner and doctor—drove madly through a Portland neighborhood with the husband of a woman whom, he said, was in labor and dying. During the drive, two women signaled frantically from a curb to summon Dr. Adair. When she pulled up, they rushed to her side of the buggy and whispered, "Bethena, do you know you're hatless?"

Back then, the importance of women covering their heads in public could not be overemphasized.

Mrs. Kittie Strobel was one of Tacoma's most skilled milliners, and like Dr. Adair, she learned by observing. She regularly went to hat stores during their grand openings and studied what she saw. Armed with nothing but her observations and skill with a needle, she went to work as an apprentice to a woman named Mrs. M.H. Berry. Mrs. Berry gave Kittie four hats a year in lieu of a salary. From Mrs. Berry, Kittie went to work for a Miss McCutcheon, earning five dollars a week.

Because Portland was bigger than Tacoma, Kittie and her employer regularly took the train south to look at for new styles and patterns and to visit wholesale houses. They returned with silk, velvet and feathers and sewed like crazy to make new hats and refurbish old ones. In Puyallup, they displayed their work in glass cases at the Puyallup Fair. And once or twice a year, they traveled up to the foothills of Mount Rainier to sell their wares at coal mining towns such as Buckley, Carbonado and Wilkeson. When Kittie and Miss McCutcheon arrived at the first town, they'd find a place to stay and then go door-to-door, passing out handbills. The beauty-starved women flocked to their hotel. When they'd sold all they could at the first town, they rented a horse-drawn wagon and drove to others. Most of their customers couldn't speak English and brought their children to translate. Kittie said that they always came back "loaded with greenbacks."

A lady and her hat.

At that time, when large hats were back in style, women wore huge ones known as the Merry Widow, and men didn't like them. They particularly didn't like them being worn on the streetcars. Three men not only complained to officials of the Tacoma Traction Company but also filed charges. They wanted damages for things such as broken glasses, facial scratches and at least one broken derby, all caused, they claimed, by Merry Widows. Some men thought that women who wore large hats should have to pay double, but the traction company wasn't willing to go that far.

Tacoma men had other issues with the ribbons, felt and feathers that adorned the Merry Widows. They claimed that the masses of furbelows obstructed vision. Tacoma city council members decided they were right and ordered a series of fines ranging from five to ten dollars "to be levied for wearing a hat in a theater or other place of public entertainment." The ladies were furious. Fashion was fashion, and where, at the theater, were they supposed to put their hats?

And then the men tried to take the law one step further: enforce it at church services. That one didn't work; the official reason given was that because of the separation of church and state, they had no authority over churches. The unofficial one was that a big hat provided a handy shield behind which a man could doze.

Meanwhile, Kittie Strobel got married. Unusual for the time, her husband said she could continue working, if she wanted, as long as he remained the provider for the household (and presumably as long as she did all the household chores).

One day, Susan Graham Jacobi, who lived and had a millinery shop in the Winthrop Hotel, ran an ad for a trimmer. Kittie applied and was immediately hired. Every morning, Mrs. Jacobi came down from her apartment and went to her office on the balcony to go over the books. Then she went to the sales room to chat with customers. Jacobi's made hats for all Tacoma's most prominent women. Mrs. W.R. Rust, whose husband established the Tacoma Smelting & Refining Company, sent her chauffeur to the shop to pick up a selection of hats and take them back to her home for inspection. He then returned those that she didn't buy.

Kittie stayed with Mrs. Jacobi until she was seventy-six and then retired. By that time, the custom of wearing hats was going out of style. The reason given rests with the military during World War II. Photographs of dashing aviators, hatless but wearing newly developed sunglasses known as Ray Bans, put paid to headgear.

Tacoma's men also had issues with women's dresses. According to one editorialist, dressmakers were so skilled that they were able to take several yards of fabric and cut and stitch it so that a woman appeared to be wearing tights, which were illegal, without actually breaking the law. Again, the city council members weighed in. First, they ordered all posters of scantily clad

Watch those hands!

or nude burlesque dancers taken down. Then, they cast their hairy eyeballs on the two statues of nymphs in Wright Park. "It is certainly not unwarranted," one newspaper claimed, "that the ankles of these dancing girls are such as to justify their demolition"—the entire statue, not just the ankles.

The statues survived, and the men moved on to take up the issue of flirting in church. And not only that, they accused homemakers of refusing to take their servants to church for fear people would ask, "Which is the mistress and which is the maid?" Women, of course, hotly denied both these allegations. They most certainly did not flirt in church, and their servants were welcome to attend. Household help was hard to come by. A group of ladies had gone to a slum neighborhood and tried to entice some of the young women living there away from their fast-and-loose lifestyles. Unfortunately, the wages these ladies offered didn't compare favorably with the wages of sin.

And then, because the council members seemed to spend a lot of time looking at women, they created a dancing rule. "The lady, in dancing, shall place her left hand on her partner's arm and not on his back or shoulder." Men were allowed to accommodate themselves if "they had a short arm and/or a buxom dance partner."

According to the *New York Times*, which felt called upon to report the new dance rule, "The unhappy part of the situation is that the dance has fallen from the high estate of the days of the polka and schottische."

How much attention women paid to these rules isn't known. For the most part, they were too busy running their homes to bother. Suffice it to say, city council members seemed to have too much time on their hands.

Civilized Living

CLEANLINESS—NEXT TO GODLINESS?

Tacoma is going to have a city bathhouse. No doubt the municipality needs one.
—*The* Olympian

In 1972, Tacoma pioneer Ruby Blackwell looked back to the 1880s and her family's home at 1110 A Street:

> *The lavatory was off the bedroom, containing a "set"—wash bowl and toilet. Water was piped into the house from John Burns Springs on E Street. Uncle Will devised sufficient pressure for water in the bathroom by putting an oak barrel on stilts in the corner. Of course, the tub was galvanized iron. Waste was taken care of by a cesspool under the garden as there were no sewers yet.*

Miss Blackwell was wrong about Tacoma not having sewers. Community sewers constructed in 1880 ran down Pacific Avenue—the shortest route to the tidewaters of Commencement Bay. The pipes were wood, and when one broke, it was discovered that the system had no bottom. Sewage mostly remained where it was deposited.

When Miss Blackwell wrote that water in the family bathroom was stored in a barrel supported by stilts, she didn't say whether the water was for the commode or for bathing. However, people generally bathed only once a week and shampooed their hair less frequently because soaps left a dull film, making hair uncomfortable and unhealthy looking. Also, since the first commercial deodorant, Mum, wasn't patented until 1888, clearly the late nineteenth and early twentieth centuries were smelly times. One solution was public baths.

Back then, bathing meant swimming to most people. On March 18, 1891, the *Tacoma Daily News* reported that John Nannary's death was the result of bathing and that he had probably hit his head when diving into a pool. To James Tait, however, bathing meant getting clean.

Tait dropped into the *Tacoma Daily Ledger* office one day "with a roll of stiff brown paper as big around as a common stovepipe under his arm." He commandeered a desk, spread the paper out and said that for months he had been trying to come up with a way to provide the people of Tacoma with a public bathing facility.

"In nearly every city in the Union of the size of Tacoma," he said, "public baths have been established and in a general way intimating that it would be a good idea to open a first-class bathing house here, I thought it about time for me to strike out."

Tait was born in England, where twenty years earlier he had managed a public bathhouse. In Tacoma, he worked for the city as a civil engineer. Tait and architect C.A. Milligan had been bathing every week in the Puyallup River, and the two came up with the idea for the public bath.

As the plans showed, their building would be ninety by fifty-five feet on the outside and sixty-six by forty-five on the inside. The men planned a brick foundation and double-thick brick walls up to the edge of the foundation and then wood from there on. The bathing pool ranged from four and a half feet to seven and a half feet. The deep end was to have a springboard for diving. The plans included an office, boiler room and fourteen dressing rooms with locks. Their plan was to build it on the A Street bluff near Ninth Street and pump up salt water from the bay. Fresh water, Mr. Tait said, "wasn't seen as advisable."

A lady and her bath.

On ladies' days, a female matron would be in charge. On children's days, the water level would be lowered. In winter, the pool would be converted into an ice-skating rink. No one explained why keeping clean was only a summer activity.

Mr. Tait needed something, though—$6,000 to get started. The bathhouse was never built.

The cleanest people in town back then were the Japanese. Kenjo Kametaro came to town in 1906 and worked as a logger for two years. After that, he opened a barbershop and bathhouse at 1503½ Commerce Street and was both the president and treasurer of the barbers' guild and board member of the Tacoma Japanese Association.

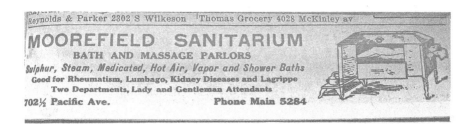

Advertisement for the Moorfield Sanitarium.

Two years later, Niiyama Shuzo came to Tacoma. He was also a board member of the Tacoma Japanese Association and president of the Tacoma Japanese Barbers' Union. In addition to a bathhouse, barbershop and laundry, he started a hotel and a combination arts/variety/clock shop.

Ishida Kaname came to town in 1912 and started a barbershop. He soon became vice-president of the barbers' union, councilor of the Japanese Association and owner of a barbershop, laundry and bathhouse at 1154 Commerce Street.

These baths were for the Japanese clientele; white Tacoma residents had their own: C.C. Swanson's Baths at 915 South Tenth Street, the Sanitorium [*sic*] Baths at 5424–26 South Puget Sound Avenue, an unnamed bathhouse at 5040 South K Street, the Royal Baths at 116 South Ninth and the Moorfield Turkish Bath in the Colonial Hotel at 701–05 Commerce Street. However, the most well known and most notorious was the Hamman Baths.

The Hamman Baths started out as a legitimate enterprise under a Pacific Avenue barbershop. It opened on December 17, 1890, with F. Fritz Keeble, a well-known "tonsorial artist" (barber) as manager. A brief article in the *Tacoma Daily News* described the baths as "handsomely decorated and fitted up with all the newest appliances." The baths were open both day and night and had accommodations for men and women. Amenities included "after-the-bath, spacious and airy cooling and lounging departments, Turkish and Russian massages, a gymnasium, a 14 ft. x 40 ft. swimming pool, and a female attendant to shampoo women's hair." The floor was covered with hexagonally shaped ceramic tiles in red, green, purple, white and ochre. The walls were tiled up approximately five feet with rectangular-shaped white tiles. Support columns were encased in marble. Mostly, the bath seemed to attract loggers. And then, in 1901, Tacoma's prostitution vice lord, Peter Sandberg, bought the facility.

Sandberg added three floors and reopened it in 1902 as the Kentucky Liquor Store. When he doubled the building's size in 1909, the address became 1128 Pacific Avenue. Sandberg took out a liquor license in 1911, and not long after, a sixteen-year-old "country girl" was wooed into the facility. The unnamed teenager told the police that she had come to town to shop and met a "sociable woman" named May Brown at a five-and-ten-cent store on C Street (Broadway) who took an interest in her. The woman suggested that she stay in town and see some picture shows, and then her new hostess invited the girl to stay overnight with her. The girl phoned her mother, after which the two went to dinner and the shows. They ended up on the seventh floor of the Kentucky. There the teenager saw "kimono-wearing girls, bottles of beer and whiskey"—and a connecting door in her room through which two men appeared saying "they were there for romance."

After several hours of the girl's refusing both the liquor and the romance, the police knocked at the door, and May Brown had the girl roll under the bed and told her to keep still. May, it turned out, was well known to the police, and when they searched, they found the teenager. The girl was the third to disappear from Tacoma's streets, and blame was placed on Sandberg's procuring methods.

Sandberg's liquor license was revoked in January 1912 and re-granted by accident eleven months later. It was a well-known fact that Sandberg made payoffs to various police officers and elected officials. A man named Edward Ackerman bought out a fellow named James Kelley and applied for a transfer of Kelley's liquor license. A third man, A.U. Mills, approved it, and the application was snuck through with a bunch of other applications and legislation requiring approval. Mayor W.W. Seymour said, "Had he taken time to read everything he'd signed, he never would have approved a liquor license for the Kentucky Hotel."

Would that he had been more careful! Police officers raided the place in 1916 and found a stash of illegal whiskey in a compartment accessed by a trapdoor that was hidden under carpeting in the women's area.

Prohibition and the country's moral movement hit Sandberg hard. He died a poor man in 1931.

The bathhouse was uncovered in 1968 and then lost to history again until 2008. Sadly, rather than turn it into a moneymaking tourist attraction, it became a rain cistern for Pacific Plaza.

CURSED ABODE?
THE QUICK AND THE DEAD AT THE RUST HOUSE

Tacoma's most recognizable house has to be the big old Classic revival colonial home on North I Street. There are others equally elegant, but it is the Tara-like house that is most often requested on the Tour of Historic Homes. This is the house that Rust built.

William and Helen Rust and their son, Howard, came to Tacoma in 1889 from Colorado. Mr. Rust was in the smelting and refining business, and he came here to buy the Tacoma Mill and Smelting Co. After the purchase, he spent a year remodeling and upgrading the facility. Eventually, Mr. Rust's smelter became the largest in the Pacific Northwest.

Mr. Rust ran the facility for fifteen years. In 1905, famed financier Bernard Baruch negotiated a deal in which Mr. Rust sold it to the Guggenheims. With a portion of the proceeds, he bought eight lots on North I Street on which to build a family home. What he apparently chose to ignore was that part of the land had belonged to embezzler Paul Schultz. And Schultz had committed suicide as the way out of his mess.

Ignoring the property's taint, Mr. Rust decided the house would be a replica, on a significantly reduced scale, of Shadow Lawn, the home owned by New York businessman John A. McCall. Shadow Lawn had 130 rooms and the Rust mansion 18. And Shadow Lawn was built from Indiana limestone; the Rust home was built from Wilkeson sandstone. But hey, that was huge for Tacoma, and there were similarities in the floor plan.

The first floor of the house that Rust built had a library, a dining room, a small domed-ceiling reception room that adjoined a south veranda, a kitchen, a butler's pantry and a pergola (a walkway supported by posts and covered by latticework over which vines grow) with a northern view of Puget Sound. The family bedrooms, sitting rooms, bathrooms, dressing rooms and guest bedrooms and baths were all on the second floor. The third floor had spare guest facilities, plus the servants' bedrooms and sitting room.

Puget Sound was chock full of cedar, oak and pine, so much so that it was *déclassé*. The walls that Mr. Rust didn't cover with imported gold and green French wallpaper were oak or mahogany. There was also a vacuum cleaning system, trunk elevator and telephone intercom, a billiard room with a floor of interlocking rubber plates, a ballroom with a maple dance floor, a laundry room with a clothes dryer and furnace and fuel rooms in the basement. Altogether, Mr. Rust's home sweet home consisted of eighteen rooms, four baths and eight gas fireplaces.

The Rust House, circa 1907.

South of the house was the carriage house and north was a two-car garage, chauffeur's quarters and robe room. The garage was designed to support a summer garden. The grounds also had a sunken Italian garden.

Mr. McCall lived at Shadow Lawn for three years; the Rusts occupied their home for five years. In 1910, while William and Helen and their youngest son, Arthur, were in Europe, their oldest son, Howard, had a sudden heart attack and died. The memories of their son, in combination with such a large, empty house, were too much for Mrs. Rust. Also, a man named Samuel Glenn built "an ugly little laundry building" directly across the street. The Rusts sold their home to George Savage and W.R. Nichols, who in turn sold it to Francis Bailey. Mr. Bailey lived there a year before A.E. Grafton took it away in a foreclosure and sold it to Orville Billings, president of the Pacific Building and Loan Association, and his wife, Minnie. They partitioned off rooms and created twelve apartments to help alleviate the World War I housing shortage.

Mr. Billings lost his job when a fourteen-year-old hearing- and speech-impaired girl brought assault charges against him. Just before he was to stand trial, while in the dining room showing a new pistol to his wife and a friend, Orville Billings put it to his head and pulled the trigger. Investigating authorities came to the conclusion that Mr. Billings had been unaware there was one bullet still in the chamber, and therefore the death was an accident. However, the insurance company may have thought differently because Mrs. Billings had to sue for benefits.

Mrs. Billings sold the house to James E. Bell, and it became the Bell Mansion Apartments. In 1931, when the occupants included a family named Krueger, Fred Williams of Paramount Securities Loan Company obtained a lien against some of their furnishings for back taxes due. On Christmas Eve, Mr. Kreuger armed himself with a double-barreled shotgun and Mrs. Kreuger with a rifle. Their maid, Izotta, had a double-bitted axe, and their friends Fred Massie and Johnnie Kennedy each held revolvers. They barricaded the doors and windows and held the authorities at bay. The standoff was the excitement of the Christmas holiday that year. It was also a complicated affair that ended up in court.

To summarize, William Rust bought land that included lots previously owned by a suicide victim. The oldest Rust son died unexpectedly of a heart attack; after the Rusts moved, the second son may or may not have staged his own kidnapping. Mr. Billings died in the dining room by his own hand, and an armed siege took place at the house during the Depression.

The Rust home continued as an apartment complex until 1983, when it was purchased and returned to a single-family dwelling. So far, there have been no untold incidents.

LEAN BACK AND OPEN WIDE

For a time, Charles Spinning was Pierce County's only doctor. When people sent for him, he traveled by foot, horse or canoe and used what was at hand to treat the patient. Dr. Spinning used spider webs to stop bleeding and treated achy joints with heated slices of lily roots. He made enema bags from deer bladders or kelp. And when one of his patients complained of a toothache, Dr. Spinning had him lay on the floor, sat on the man's chest and pulled the bad tooth with a bullet mold.

Throughout history, dental procedures have been risky business. To remedy the pain caused by bad teeth, barbers/surgeons/dentists tried alcohol, chloroform, hashish, marijuana, mesmerism, exotic ointments and cocaine. Sigmund Freud was a strong proponent of cocaine, "thinking it a miraculous answer to a variety of behaviors as well as dental problems." In 1887, an unnamed reporter from the *Tacoma Daily Ledger* had a tooth pulled under the effects of cocaine and reported it to be "a happy experience."

However, pioneer settler Fred Nunns had nothing either good or bad to say about his anesthetic—and for a good reason. For several years, Fred

Dr. Spinning performs his bullet mold dental procedure. *Lenard Eccles, artist.*

treated several of his troublesome teeth with carbolic acid. One day in 1923 when he had to go to town, Fred decided to have them pulled and be done with them. The pain went away, but so did Fred. Shortly after the extractions, he died from a suspected case of Novocain overdose.

By the early twentieth century, the hypodermic needle had been substantially refined, making the use of cocaine a lot easier, but dentists weren't convinced that it was the best way to go; the results were highly unpredictable. In 1912, two local men volunteered to undergo unnecessary extractions in the interests of science. Dr. E.J. Doty sat in the midst of a group from the Pierce County Dental Association and let a fellow dentist treat him with a "mixture in the form of quinine" and pull a tooth. A second "unidentified business professional" was treated with a combination of nitrous oxide and oxygen and also had a tooth pulled. Their sacrifices were part of a national movement to find an anesthesia that was safe, reliable and non-addictive. Being painless wasn't one of their priorities.

Extractions, however, weren't the only dental problems. Gun disease was rampant. One common treatment for problem gums that lasted well into the twentieth century was the application of a leech (the best-quality leeches were believed to be those imported from the Dalmatian coast) to the affected area. A leech practitioner coaxed the worm into a leech tube, the patient held the end of the tube against the infected gum for twenty to thirty minutes and the leech nibbled away. It was a procedure requiring patience, care and a firm, steady hand because it wasn't unknown for a "lively leech to escape from the tube and start down the patient's throat."

And then there were false teeth. They date to 700 BC, when Etruscans made dentures from human or animal teeth. At about the same time, the Japanese were making wooden dentures. Porcelain teeth came in the 1770s with Wedgewood providing most of the porcelain paste. Over the years, dentists experimented with elk or cow teeth and walrus or elephant tusks. Battleground scavenging for teeth was common from the Civil War through the various Indian wars. Those who couldn't afford dentures had three choices: do without teeth altogether; stuff rolls of cloth between the cheek and gum to fill out the space, as Queen Elizabeth I did; or try to find some comfortable dentures. Interestingly enough, the dentures weren't for eating; they were for wearing out in public. To eat, people either hid in another room and gummed their food or invested in a masticator. Dental supply catalogues sold masticators, and some cookbooks even suggested them with their recipes. Smart mothers may well have used them to pre-chew food for their babies.

For as long as soldiers used muskets, the military required its soldiers to have at least two teeth—an upper and corresponding lower—so they could tear open the paper patch. During World War I, at the request of a Camp Lewis medical officer, the following inquiry was sent to the provost marshal general: "Medical officer assigned to this department asks to be advised whether contemplated scope of dental work referred to (in section 185) includes bridge and plate work."

An answer came back saying, "Men who are otherwise physically fit but would need dental bridge or plate work in order to have the mastication requirements set forth in the regulations (four molars that met) would have to take care of their dental problems themselves."

Edgar "Painless" Parker was a well-known pioneer dentist. The "mogul of the mouth" was as much a showman as a man of dentistry. He took medicine shows on the road using troupes of actors, singers, acrobats, jugglers, magicians and tap dancers to attract business. Detractors said his principal anesthetic was noise and confusion. Nevertheless, he opened a chain of clinics around the country. His Brooklyn clinic had a ten-foot-tall advertising sign. His Tacoma clinic, located at 1101–03 Broadway, was on the second floor, and the sign was about two feet tall.

On August 14, 1939, Dr. Paul Hallock of 5401 South Tacoma Way retired thirty years to the minute after beginning his dental practice. When leaving his office, he took with him a box containing every tooth he'd ever pulled. He said he was thinking about incorporating them in a barbecue he was building.

SILENT STEEDS: RECREATIONAL WHEELS

In 1888, thirty-seven men organized the Tacoma Wheelman, a bicycling club that met in the Davis Building (since demolished) at 910–12 Pacific Avenue. Not long after, the women organized the Ladies' Bicycle Club. The men assumed a uniform that included knee pants, and most of the women went for bloomers. Both clubs were united in their frustration over Tacoma's plank roads.

The club members were a little behind the time when it came to biking. Safety bikes hadn't made it to Tacoma yet, and the wheelmen rode something nicknamed the boneshaker. It had a wooden frame and wheels and pedals attached to a large front iron tire.

By 1895, tough safety bicycles were becoming commonplace. They had equal-sized wheels, pedals attached to a sprocket through gears and a chain. Additional innovations included hollow steel tubing, coaster brakes and adjustable handlebars.

The bikers' aims were threefold: for the members to ride their own bikes, to teach others to ride and work to get decent bike-riding roads. They wanted a network of paths from ten to fifteen feet wide and surfaced with cinders "so as to be suitable for riding throughout the city and beyond." One of their first projects was to improve the old water ditch road that ran along the Clover Creek flume from the Twenty-eighth and G Streets reservoir to the prairie. The club raised $300 and improved the road for five miles. The improvement was a mixed blessing. It gave cyclers a road out to the country but also gave them views of ducks, cows and children frolicking in the city's drinking water. Undoubtedly, however, the men's greatest achievement was the Tacoma Bicycle Bridge.

Ladies take to the road.

Civilized Living

In in addition to meeting in the Davies Building, the men also had an indoor track at the Columbia Hall on the southwest corner of Ninth Street and Tacoma Avenue. The Tacoma Wheelmen sold bicycle licenses and by 1896 had enough money to pay for a wooden bridge, built on top of steel poles high above Gallagher's Gulch near Holy Rosary Church. It was 440 feet long, 127 feet high and 12 feet wide. It connected Delin Street with the paths leading to the Hood Street reservoir. The bridge opened the way for cyclists to bike undisturbed from Tacoma's east side to South Tacoma. For more than twenty-five years, it was the "longest, highest and only exclusive" bicycle bridge in the world.

Cycling became so popular that some Tacoma residents had small bike garages attached to their homes. The city imposed an annual one-dollar-per-bike tax and set speed limits of six miles per hour in the city and twelve miles per hour in residential areas. Peter C. Lawson was arrested on July 24, 1893, for riding his bicycle on the Tacoma Avenue sidewalk and hitting and cutting a little boy. He was released when it was discovered that the ordinance covering streets with sidewalks where biking was illegal didn't include Tacoma Avenue. When fines and revenues were collected, the money went toward additional trail improvements. Two years after the bridge was built, the Tacoma Police Department formed an experimental bicycle squad. A year later, it was declared a success. Not only could the beat cop cover a larger territory, but he could also do it in silence. And the local roads were in such poor condition, and the automobiles so noisy, that bike patrol officers could easily overtake them.

One day when a "dangerous resident of Western State Hospital" escaped, Dr. John Wesley Waughop "dispatched several of his men after the fugitive on bicycles." Another time, a man named Peter Pepe was surprised by "three masked highwaymen at his South K Street saloon." There was no policeman in sight when the first shots rang out, but within minutes an officer burst through the door on his bike, gun drawn. Tacoma police officers rode safety bikes until 1908, when a motorized bike patrol was created.

Uniformed employees of the Postal Telegraph Cable Company at 1105 A Street were forerunners to bicycle messengers.

During bicycle riding's peak years of popularity, every professional man and a great many women rode one. Homemakers fastened baskets to their handlebars when they went for groceries or wanted to give the baby some fresh air. W.W. Seymour, benefactor of the Wright Park Conservatory, was a familiar sight riding to social functions with the tails of his tux tucked into his back pockets for protection. A good biker could to ride to The Lakes (Lakeview) and back in two hours. People biked as far as Lake Lawrence to fish. Once, four men rode to American Lake to hunt a cougar that had disrupted a picnic the previous day. There was even a Tacoma-to-Portland race.

"Learn to ride a bicycle," Mark Twain said during the heyday of the craze. "You will not regret it—if you live"

BEHIND THE WRONG KINDS OF BARS

"Unfit for Beasts. Death Lurks in the Cells," was a headline in the *Tacoma Daily News*. The first thing an investigating reporter saw was the doorless toilet whose smell overpowered lime, iodoform and carbolic acid. Up to thirty-five prisoners shared seven cells on the first floor. Three cells on the lower level were considered too damp to use. The others were also damp but were occupied nevertheless. The day the reporter visited, a half-inch puddle of water measuring six by fifteen feet covered the floor. Overall, he was almost unable to handle the odor. Wooden bars separated a fifteen- by fifteen-foot space that constituted the women's prison. It was not unusual for prisoners to sleep on the floor and, if being released the next morning, to be sent away hungry. Nor was it unusual for unemployed laborers to ask for a place to sleep at night.

Tacoma's first jail was a small, wooded, two-cell building built out of two-by-four planks that were laid flat and spiked together. It was built around 1871 near McCarver and Starr Streets in Old Town. There was also a small police station at North Twelfth and G Streets, and both of these were eventually moved, first to the Old Town Wharf at the foot of Starr Street and again, in the 1890s, to the bluff at North Thirtieth and Starr. The Old Town jail remained in use until 1913, but people in New Tacoma needed a more convenient facility. The city built a combination police station, jail and dog pound at Twelfth Street and Cliff Avenue sometime around 1880. It was a two-story wooden building with the jail in the basement. After 1889, when Old and New Tacoma merged, it became the police headquarters building.

At the time the two Tacomas merged, there were twenty-five patrolmen, thirty saloons and twenty-one ways to lose money at Harry Morgan's Theatre Comique. When hired, rookie policemen received guns and badges but no training. Hires were often political appointees, and one mayor gave the jobs to elderly Civil War veterans. Among their duties was the task of assisting women—carrying them, if necessary—across the muddy roads.

Behind the wrong kinds of bars.

When it came to providing for the police, Tacoma's city council members were, not surprisingly, very tight-fisted. In 1890, Chief M.A. (Mart) Dillon went before the council to request a paddy wagon.

"When prisoners refuse to or are unable to walk to jail," he said, "the officers use a rusty old wheelbarrow to haul them in."

In a nineteenth-century version of political correctness, the chief was careful to point out that it wasn't just sailors, loggers and mill hands who required the wheelbarrow's services.

"The good laboring people of the city must not be overlooked," he added. "As this class of our fellow citizen had but little time for leisure, much leniency must be allowed them when known by the officers to be honest and industrious people."

A paddy wagon was a serious and expensive proposition, and one that required a lot of discussion. Then someone pointed out that Seattle had one, and that settled it. Chief Dillon got his wagon.

The wagon rolled out of the police station in June 1890. It had black sideboards and gilt lettering, two large rear wheels and two smaller front ones. It was pulled by a pair of matched roans. Eighteen years later, when the police upgraded to gas-powered automobiles, the old wagon was said to have traveled 100,000 miles and worn out twenty pairs of horses.

Next to go before the city council was Marshall E.O. Fulmer. Fulmer was there because members realized it had a potential workforce in the city jail, and why not let prisoners earn their keep by working in road gangs? Fulmer said that it could be done but that he didn't have enough men to act as guards. Rather than hire more men, the council members approved

Chief Dillon's wheelbarrow.

the purchase of leg irons. The chain gangs never did get much work done, but their presence drew crowds, and parents used them to point out the degradation as a threat to their children.

Deputy city marshal George Cavanaugh's problem was a lack of handcuffs. When he asked the council to approve their purchase, he was called before it to explain why the time-honored rope was no longer good enough. Cavanaugh explained that his request was the direct result of a neighborhood squabble in Old Women's Gulch, the current site of Stadium Bowl. Apparently, a new member of the squatters' community complained to the owner when a flock of her chickens roosted on his back porch. She told him where to go jump, and he countered with where she could go. Things got ugly, and a real knock-down-drag-out fight began. The police were called in and tried to restrain the new resident with a piece of rope. Cavanaugh pointed out how hard it was to get a rope around the hands of a man who didn't want to be tied, and the councilmen were convinced.

In 1895, a deputy who owned a Kodak camera was given the task of creating a rogue's gallery of photographs.

In 1899, the police moved to the basement of Old City Hall. There were no separate facilities for women; juvenile offenders were tossed in with hardened adult prisoners, and the smell was as bad as ever. Nine years later, some improvements were made. However, the dungeon, or "Dark Hole," remained the same and was still used to make prisoners talk.

Considering the jail facilities, it's easy to understand why the idea of even temporary residence there made the men less than cooperative.

Part IV

Comings and Goings

GET THEE TO THE BROTHEL: SARAH BERNHARDT ENTERTAINS

French tragedian Sarah Bernhardt was not an attractive woman, but she certainly didn't deserve to be mistaken for a prostitute. Nevertheless, that is what happened in Tacoma.

A performance at the one-year-old, 1,300-seat Tacoma Theater was part of a worldwide trip that had already taken the actress to Australia and British Columbia. At 2:00 p.m. on the afternoon of September 23, 1891, a wooden railroad sled pulled a twelve-car chartered train onto a siding at Seventeenth Street and Pacific Avenue, where a crowd had gathered to welcome the thespian.

While Madame Sarah; her son, Maurice, and daughter-in-law, Princess Therese Jablonowska; and traveling companion, Mademoiselle Suzanne Seylor, slipped away for a carriage ride through the business district, a reporter from the *Tacoma Daily Ledger* visited her train. Besides the engine and caboose, it consisted of three Pullman sleepers, five baggage and scenery cars and several private coaches, he wrote. Her manager, Henry E. Abbey, his wife and a maid traveled in the Hazelmere, and the Divine Sarah, Maurice and his princess wife, who was generally referred to as Countess Terka, and Mademoiselle Seylor rode in the Coronet; other members rode in the Alcatraz. One of those other members was a French chef who regularly prepared five-course dinners for the company.

The Tacoma Theater, circa 1907.

The *Ledger* reporter devoted a full paragraph to Mr. Abbey's appearance, courage and sagacity and two lines to Madame Bernhardt, saying, "She talks rapidly and earnestly, gesticulating the while. She is not handsome or even attractive looking."

Things started going wrong for the actress in the late afternoon of her first day in town. After the carriage ride, Madam Sarah, who carried a gun and was accompanied by a dog, Maurice, the princess and Mademoiselle Seylor, decided to visit Wright Park, which had just been logged and replanted with deciduous trees. On their way back downtown, they got lost. Who better to ask directions of than a policeman? Sadly, the policeman they asked wasn't a fan of theater, or he didn't speak French or he didn't like the cut of their jib. For whatever reason, he directed them to Harry Morgan's Theatre Comique, a disreputable bawdy house that, at the time, was featuring, "Forty Beautiful Ladies." Thirty years earlier, when Madame Bernhardt had applied for a job in burlesque, she was turned down. And she wasn't about to make a career change and join Morgan's ladies at this late date. She found her way to Ninth Street and eventually back to her train.

The next thing to go wrong had to do with the theater programs. When Madame arrived at the theater, she waited in her "copay" and sent her valet to find the manager, a man named Heilig. When he came out, he saw that the actress was in shock, and not from the afternoon's misunderstanding. And he also quickly learned that she wasn't the sweet little thing she played on stage. Madame Sarah shrieked a "monosyllabic, stentorian soliloquy of prefatory expletives." Mr. Heilig rushed to the door of her coupe. "Tell me," he implored, "what has happened?"

All Madame could do was point at the program, where on the first page were printed the following words: "Bonnie Kate Castleton—The Dazzler— Full of Ginger Start to Finish."

"Is zis not an ensult to ze great Sarah to put zees Dazzlaire in ze program when Sarah eez here?" the newspaper wrote in its version of French-accented English. "Ake him out, toot sweet, or I do not play tonight."

After her grand announcement, Madame was assisted to her dressing room and helped to a sofa, where "she lay gasping and sobbing and plucking out her hair in a wild and foreign way."

As he stood a distance away, manager Heilig was heard to mutter, "I'll have no more foreign stars."

Nevertheless, the play, *Fedora*, went on—four acts of "turgid tragedy about nihilist violence in St. Petersburg and Paris." The *Ledger*'s critic called the play "brutal" and Madame Bernhardt "perfect."

And then she was gone, leaving town before reading some of the spectators' comments. To wit:

"Why should she speak in French all the time?"

"Of course I went to see Sarah Bernhardt last evening. It was not that I cared so much to see her, but as everybody else was going, I went to see them."

"I resent it. I do not understand French, and I don't want to pay four or five dollars for something I cannot understand."

And another comment from Mr. Heilig: "Nobody is great to his own valet."

The next time she appeared in Tacoma, though Madame was more appreciated, she unfortunately met up with Murphy's Law. The date was June 13, 1913, and she was acknowledged as being "long past her prime." For this performance, she did the last act of *Camille*, and again she spoke entirely in French, but the *Tacoma Times* theater critic said "she held the audience in a spell."

No, the problem wasn't her French or her performance; it was her accommodations. Madame asked for seven rooms: a parlor, bedroom and bath for herself, a room for her physician and three for servants. Unfortunately, the Masons and the Catholic Foresters were both holding conventions in Tacoma. There was "no room at the inn," or at least not the kinds of rooms she wanted. In the end, Madame Sarah stayed in Seattle and was driven down to entertain.

Sarah Bernhardt died ten years later. Her problems in Tacoma played no part in her demise.

EXPLETIVES DELETED: MARK TWAIN IN TACOMA

Mark Twain didn't want to come west. He was a few months short of sixty and had a hacking cough, aching bones and a giant carbuncle (a large pus-filled abscess deep in the skin). He was $320,000 in debt (more than $1 million

today), and his publishing company had just failed. Someone suggested that every person in the country send him a nickel to help out; however, both Mr. and Mrs. Twain said, "Thanks but no thanks." They, alone, would pay their debts. This in spite of Twain's close friend and business advisor, H.H. Rogers of the Standard Oil Company, who told the humorist that he couldn't think of a single man he knew older than fifty-eight who had been able to recover from financial failure.

And so Twain and his manager, Major J.B. Pond, decided Twain would make a round-the-world trip giving a talk called, "Ninety Minutes of Chat and Character Sketches."

Mark Twain wearing his "don'tcareadamn suit."

The Twains, their daughter,

Clara, and Major and Mrs. Pond left Elmira, New York, on July 14, 1895, and headed west; first stop, Cleveland, where the tour began the next day. From Cleveland, it was on to Sault Ste. Marie, Mackinac and Petoskey, Michigan; Duluth, Minneapolis and St. Paul, Minnesota; Winnipeg, Manitoba; back to Crookston, Minnesota; on to Great Falls, Butte, Anaconda, Helena and Missoula, Montana; Spokane, Washington; Portland, Oregon; and then back to Washington at Olympia, Tacoma, Seattle and New Whatcom, to be followed by Vancouver and Victoria, British Columbia. Twain had given nineteen talks in the twenty-seven days before he hit Tacoma.

Ill health plagued Twain much of the way, and he missed many dinners that had been planned in his honor. But he played to packed houses, sometimes over one thousand people at a time, and at the end of the U.S. leg of his tour, he was able to remit some $5,000 to his creditors.

Just about everywhere Twain went, the newspapers commented on his appearance. Lute Pease of the *Portland Oregonian* wrote that he wore "a blue nautical cap which confined a part of his big mane of hair, which bulged out at the sides and behind—a grizzly wilderness."

A reporter for the *Tacoma Morning Union* said, "Twain's hair seemed to be dressed very much like Ophelia's hair after she loses her mental reckoning."

Twain was packing a dress suit at the Fairhaven Hotel and was only half dressed when he received a reporter from the *New Whatcom Blade*. The reporter's opinion was that Twain's shaggy head of hair reminded him of "one of the Albino freaks with a little black pepper thrown in."

The general agreement among the various newspapers, though, was that Mark Twain didn't look like a funny man.

The *Morning Union* noted that Twain wore brown socks and brown velvet slippers with his dark suit. For those interested in palmistry, the paper printed the front and backs of his hands. Seeing this, Twain said that "some readers of his palm, not knowing his identity, had described him as troubled by excessive alcoholism, as a man easily swayed by the ladies, a vigorous individualist liable to lose money, and a person with absolutely no sense of humor."

As the touring party approached the Pacific Northwest, Twain was quite frankly apprehensive. For one thing, the area was still recovering from the 1893 Financial Panic. John D. Rockefeller had withdrawn his investments from Everett; fourteen banks in Seattle and twenty-one in Tacoma had failed. Sixteen hundred Puget Sound men were getting ready to march on Washington, D.C., to urge public works programs. Forest fires had been raging in virgin timber throughout the Olympic Peninsula. The country was gripped by a severe drought, and heavy smoke lay on the water. The inland air was so smoke filled that at times it obscured the sun. And he faced plenty of competition. In Seattle, HMS *Pinafore* was playing at Madison Park; Leschi Park had a concert by the First Regimental Band and Madrona Park was holding a nightly electric fountain exhibition.

Tacoma was working on plans for an upcoming tennis tournament and was heavily involved in the baseball rivalry with Seattle. In Olympia, the Woman's Christian Temperance Union was holding its annual convention. Vice President Adlai B. Stevenson was in the area, and an alleged sea serpent had been sighted in the bay.

Twain and party traveled from Seattle to Tacoma on the steamboat *Flyer*, with Twain complaining most of the way. He referred to the baggage handlers as baggage smashers and quite frankly wished his luggage was filled with dynamite that would "blow them all to kingdom come." But then, before the *Flyer* docked, he encountered an old friend, Lieutenant Commander Wadhams, who invited him to dinner aboard the USS *Mohican*, and after arriving in Tacoma, he renewed a friendship with Mrs. Frank Allyn, who hosted a tea for the writer and his wife and daughter. For a little while, at least, things looked up.

The group stayed at the Tacoma Hotel, and Mark Twain spoke at the Tacoma Theater on August 12, 1895. The *Tacoma Daily Ledger* described his talk as "not exactly a lecture nor yet readings." They were "odd little tales of no particular moral but having a point." The *Tacoma Daily News* said that "some of the audience was unable to swing into line with Mark's particular line of humor and they looked tired, too tired even to smile." Nevertheless, most of the audience roared with laughter, and when they did, the humorist "pulled his moustache and scowled."

He was even more entertaining at the Tacoma Press Club banquet held later that evening. Using his I-used-to-be-a-newspaperman-myself persona, Twain and the men swapped stories until long after midnight. When an Olympia man apologized for the heavy smoke, Twain said, "I don't mind so much. I am accustomed to it. I am a perpetual smoker myself." When Major Pond said this was his fourth visit to Puget Sound and he had yet to see a single mountain, Twain responded, "But really, your scenery is wonderful. It's quite out of sight." When the major commented on Clara Clemens's skill on the piano, Twain explained modestly that it was transmitted genius. Ever the diplomat, in Seattle he called the mountain Rainier and in Tacoma, Tacoma.

For the time he was here, Puget Sound newspapers were full of stories about the great American humorist, but Twain himself seemed to remember little about the Pacific Northwest. Writing *Following the Equator*, published in 1897, he made particular note of his relief in finally setting sail and his pleasure in the "enticing and welcome sea after the distressful dustings and smokings and swelterings of the past few weeks."

So You Want to Be a Star?
Hollywood Beckons

Movies were almost an obsession by the mid-1920s. Theater owners changed their playbills on Mondays and Fridays, which meant that a movie had a three-day life expectancy. Silent films didn't require stage-trained actors as the talkies soon would. An attractive face and a lot of hyperbolic body language sufficed. Low-budget westerns and stunt and action thrillers were the bread-and-butter of the business, and the studios were turning out nearly 750 films a year. With such seemingly favorable odds, young people poured into Hollywood hoping for stardom—and the numbers included several Tacoma women.

Mildred Davis—"Mid," as she was known—was born in Philadelphia in 1900 and for a few years attended a Quaker grade school there. The Davises came to Tacoma when Mid was still young enough to attend Lowell Grade School. From Lowell, Mid went to Annie Wright Seminary and Stadium High School. Her education included training in classical dance, and she developed a great love of theater.

After high school, Mid went back east to attend college. While there, her photograph ended up in the hands of a couple of Los Angeles movie directors. They thought she had Mary Pickford potential and suggested that she go to California for screen tests. Mid tested well and landed a movie role. For a few years, she made movies for Metro, Pathe and Mutual Studios. But eventually, she decided that her film career was over and returned to Tacoma.

In the meantime, a New Yorker named Hal Roach was kicking around the Pacific Northwest and Alaska. When he came into a small inheritance, Roach used it to start Hal Roach Studios in Los Angeles. He hired a bit player named Harold Lloyd and told him to come up with a comedy persona comparable to either that of Charlie Chaplin's Little Tramp or Buster Keaton's deadpan expression. Harold went to work and developed a character, the forerunner to PBS's Mr. Bean, an ordinary man who becomes involved in extraordinary circumstances. Tortoise-rimmed glasses were his main prop and identification.

Hollywood Boulevard in the movies' Golden Years.

Roach and Lloyd made a lot of one-reel comedies, many of which featured leading lady Bebe Daniels. Eventually, Miss Daniels left the Roach studios to make dramatic films for Cecil B. DeMille. The hunt was on for a new leading lady.

One day, Roach and Lloyd saw a movie called *Weaver of Dreams* starring blond-haired and blue-eyed Mildred Davis. The men decided that she was just what they were looking for. There was just one little problem: they couldn't find her! Lloyd contacted various producers, sent telegrams to his contacts and even ran newspaper ads. Finally, he hired private detectives, who traced Mildred to Tacoma. Both men hightailed it up to convince the actress to return to pictures. When they got here, however, what they saw was not what they wanted. Instead of the tomboy street urchin they'd seen on screen, they found a lovely young woman who wore elegant dresses and liked fancy hairstyles. In addition to that, Mid's father didn't think much of movie stars and wanted his daughter to stay in Tacoma and get a "real job." Facing an uphill battle, Roach and Lloyd used the ultimate weapon: money. Mid returned to Hollywood with their promise of high wages and her promise to them to return to her boyish, urchin image. With her went kid brother Jack, who was hired as the villain in eleven episodes of the *Our Gang* comedy series.

Comings and Goings

Mildred Davis was Harold Lloyd's leading lady in fifteen comedies made in the 1920s. The most well known was *Safety Last,* which featured a memorable scene of Lloyd dangling high above the street from the hands of a clock.

Mid was not only Harold Lloyd's leading lady on the screen, but she also became his leading lady in real life. Harold used to say that he married her to keep her from going to another studio.

The famous pair and their children returned to Tacoma often to see friends and family, and those same family and friends really liked to return the visits. Over the years, the Lloyds amassed a fortune. They built a twenty-five-room house on twenty-two acres in Beverly Hills and put in a nine-hole golf course, a handball court and an eight-hundred-foot canoe stream that included a waterfall and pool. In typical Hollywood style, however, their marriage wasn't always smooth sailing. Lloyd was both an unfaithful husband and a workaholic, and Mildred suffered from depression and bouts of alcoholism. One of her closest friends was Marion Davies, William Randolph Hearst's actress/mistress and no stranger to the attractions of John Barleycorn herself. Nevertheless, the Lloyds' forty-six-year marriage may be a Tinsel Town record.

Mildred Davis died in 1969, and Harold Lloyd followed in 1971. Initially, the studios may have been looking for a Mary Pickford knock-off, but they got something better: a woman who achieved her own on-screen success and whose career outlasted that of Pickford.

Wanda Hawley was another local girl who found success in silent films. She was born in Scranton, Pennsylvania, on July 30, 1897, but her family moved to the Puget Sound when she was a child. She went to high school in Bremerton and then attended the Master School of Music in Brooklyn and the University of Washington. Her studies in piano and composing led to a concert tour of the United States and Canada. Wanda was living in Tacoma, either on South Seventh and Ainsworth or South Ninth and Grant (newspaper articles differ), when she decided to give Hollywood a try.

Wanda, whose real name was Selma Wanda Pittack, made her debut in 1917 with the William Fox Company. She then joined the Famous Players-Lasky Studio and was Douglas Fairbanks's leading lady in *Mr. Fix-It.* She worked for Cecil B. DeMille and acted with some of the most famous leading men of the time: Wallace Reid, William S. Hart and Rudolph Valentino, among others. She was Realart Studio's most important star and was one of the biggest stars of the silent era, receiving more fan mail than Gloria Swanson.

Wanda's acting career ended with the advent of the talkies. Her second career was as a San Francisco call girl. She died in 1963.

Tacoma newspapers had a number of articles about Juanita Hansen, but they don't say where, in Tacoma, she lived. Juanita was born on March 3, 1895, in Des Moines, Iowa, became a Sennett Bathing Beauty and stared in a number of serials, such as *The Lost Jungle*, during the teen years of the twentieth century. *The Lost Jungle*'s fifteen episodes were run at Tacoma's Pantages Theater in November and December 1920. Juanita particularly remembered that film because the animals employed weren't well trained, and she was painfully scratched by a leopard during filming. Other serials she made were *The Jungle Princess*, *The Phantom Foe* and *The Yellow Arm*. She also made two Oz movies, *The Magic Cloak of Oz* and *The Patchwork Girl of Oz*. However, Juanita's fast-and-loose lifestyle and subsequent cocaine addiction overwhelmed her. In 1924, she wrote a series of articles published in the *Tacoma Daily Ledger* telling how she was introduced to and became addicted to "Gutter Glitter."

Juanita made her first and last talkie in 1933. After that, she did some live theater. In 1938, she wrote a book, *The Conspiracy of Silence*, in which she advocated treatment instead of jail time for addicts. Juanita's habit ate up all her money, and during the Depression she worked for the Works Progress Administration. Nevertheless, in Hollywood's version of destitute, it was her maid who found the actress's body in her West Hollywood home on February 11, 1961.

Opera singer Valentine Grant, born on February 14, 1881, was a member of Tacoma's Ladies' Musical Club when she went to New York in 1913. One day she was singing for the Metropolitan Opera, and the next day she had disappeared, leaving the Met in the lurch. A couple months later, she turned up in Jacksonville, Florida, as a member of Sid Olcott's International Players. She was the heroine in a serial called *When Men Would Kill*, the story of a Florida feud. She became Olcott's companion and acted in his film *Nan o' the Backwoods* and starred in *All for Old Ireland*. She was also in movies made by the Lubin Studios and Famous Players-Lasky. Valentine married Olcott, and after appearing in a few more films, she retired in 1918.

Minerva O'Callaghan was a young Tacoma homemaker with a four-year-old son when she made the startling discovery that her life held an "endless eternity of dirty dishes." So she packed up and moved to California with a younger sister. Minerva wrote a lengthy article for the *Tacoma Daily Ledger* in which she described the process she undertook in order to get into the movies. Minerva did act, at least once for the Goldwyn Studio and also for Famous Players-Lasky, but she isn't listed under O'Callaghan as a silent screen actress.

Samaria Outouse, who lived at 2106 North Steele Street, was a University of Washington junior when she won a Metro-Goldwyn-Meyer screen test in 1928. She isn't listed anywhere, either, so apparently the test wasn't successful.

Proving, then as now, going Hollywood isn't all skittles and beer.

IT STARTED AT WARNER BROTHERS: ART GILMORE

There was a time when Art Gilmore's voice was so familiar to radio listeners, TV watchers or moviegoers that he needed no introduction. His was the voice of hundreds of announcements. "It wasn't especially deep like some announcers," Leonard Maltin once said, "but it had authority, command and yet also a kind of friendliness. I think it was an all-American voice."

And that voice grew up in Tacoma.

Art was born on March 18, 1912. He went to Washington Grade School, Jason Lee Jr. High and Stadium High School. Radio was just developing, and Art loved it. He was only fourteen when he built his own broadcasting set. And he could also sing, which he did at recitals and weddings and in concerts.

From high school, Art went to the College (now the University) of Puget Sound for a year and then transferred to the University of Washington. He became an executive officer on a Sea Scouts ship commanding twenty boys on a voyage to Vancouver and worked as an announcer at KWSC radio and as a dishwasher. In one of those Schwab Drugstore stories, someone heard him singing to the dishes and asked him if he wanted to be a star. Art quit college, sold insurance during the day and sang with dance bands at night. He began a five-year study of voice, and in between studying, selling insurance and performing at nightclubs, he sang in church choirs and for anyone who would hire him or at any place where he could pick up a few bucks. However, when Art got a job at KVI radio in Tacoma, it was a step toward the big time.

While tracking down an insurance prospect, Art heard that the station was looking for a radio announcer. He talked himself into applying and then convinced the station manager that anyone who could sell in person, as he was doing with insurance, could certainly do the same thing over a microphone. The manager hired Art for the princely sum of fifteen dollars a

Warner Brothers Studio in the early 1900s.

month, and the duties included singing, reading poetry, introducing various acts and announcing the Hollywood news. Art was so good that KOL radio in Seattle hired him away from KVI.

In 1936, Art Gilmore and his friend, Maurice Webster, went to Los Angeles, and while Maurice seems to have disappeared into history, Art hit the big time in Hollywood. As luck would have it, he learned of an opening for an announcer's job at KNX. After repeated auditions, KNX, a CBS affiliate, hired him, and he remained on staff there until 1941. After that, he freelanced.

Some of the shows Art was the announcer for are pretty much forgotten: *Stars Over Hollywood*, *America's Home Front*, *What's on Your Mind?* and *Dr. Pepper*, for example. Others, such as *Red Ryder* and *Amos 'n' Andy* are still remembered. Art was the announcer for the *Ford Sunday Evening Hour* and the Los Angeles Philharmonic. Warner Brothers Studios hired him to provide narration on a number of shorts it was producing, two of which were *Power Behind the Nation* and the *Cradle of the Republic*. *Joe McDoakes* was a series of one-reel comedy shorts released between 1942 and 1956. Titles included *So You Want to Be a*

Gambler or *So You Want to Build a House*. The show had regular guest stars such as Doris Day and Ronald Regan, with whom Art worked. He narrated Joe's humorous efforts to accomplish the activity that was the focus of the shorts until 1946.

When television came along, Art decided he'd better get ready for the new medium, at least as a salesman if nothing else, so he opened two television shops. His voice was so familiar, though, that the change of medium was no problem. Art worked as an announcer for *The George Gobel Show*, the *Red Skelton Hour* and *An Evening with Fred Astaire*. He narrated 156 episodes of *Highway Patrol* with Broderick Crawford, 39 segments of *Mackenzie's Raiders* with Richard Carlson and 41 episodes of *Men of Annapolis* with Guy Williams and Daryl Hickman. He announced "A Time for Choosing," also known as "The Speech," which was Ronald Reagan's prewritten speech, presented on a number of occasions during the 1964 U.S. presidential election campaign on behalf of Republican candidate Barry Goldwater.

Occasionally, Art was seen and not just heard. He appeared on the *Mary Tyler Moore Show*, *Adam-12*, *Emergency*, *Dragnet* and *The Waltons*. Art was Franklin Delano Roosevelt's voice in the 1942 production of *Yankee Doodle Dandy*, and he was the dramatic voice heard on literally hundreds of film trailers. Rita Hayworth's *Gilda* was one, as were *Shane*, *Born Yesterday*, *Vertigo*, *Dumbo* and *It's a Wonderful Life*.

In 1944, Art and CBS producer Glenn Middleton decided that the country needed a good book on the job of radio announcing. They created an outline, hired fellow announcer Jimmy Wallington to write a foreword and then wrote 130 pages of text on microphonic techniques. Included in the book were biographical sketches of top-draw announcers, sample scripts, voice production studies, microphone methods and practices and patter patterns. Hollywood Radio Publishers published the book, and when word of it got out, the company was flooded with inquiries. The University of Southern California hired Art to teach radio announcing, and he used his own textbook.

As an adult, there were only two occasions when Art wasn't working in show business. One was during World War II. He served as a navy fighter-director on an aircraft carrier in the Pacific from August 1943 until November 1945. The other was when he was on vacation. Art's mother and sister, Dorothy, still lived in Tacoma. Dorothy was head of the music department at Grant School.

In high school, Art met a girl named Grace Weller. They dated for eight years before marrying. Grace's family had a place on Steilacoom Lake, so

Art and Grace returned to Tacoma once a year for three or four weeks to visit family and so Art could fish. Fishing, golf, tennis, horseback riding and swimming were his hobbies. And if the name Weller sounds familiar, well, Art and Grace were aunt and uncle to Robb Weller, a radio producer who was once a host on *Entertainment Tonight*.

For a time in the 1960s, Art was president of the American Federation of Television and Radio Artists, a labor union. In 1966, Art, Ralph Edwards and Edgar Bergen founded the Pacific Pioneer Broadcasters. The 178-member organization provided an opportunity for those who had been involved in broadcasting for twenty years or more to socialize, network and honor fellow pioneer broadcasters for outstanding achievements. Five times a year, the PPB hosted luncheons at which a guest of honor was presented the Art Gilmore Career Achievement Award. During the luncheons, members and invited entertainment personalities shared personal memories of the honoree. In addition, members seventy-five or older were inducted into the Pacific Pioneer Broadcasters' Diamond Circle. Diamond Circle members were broadcasters who may not necessarily have been celebrities in the usual sense of the word but who had, nonetheless, made significant contributions to the broadcasting industry. Tom Kennedy and Nanette Fabray were two members.

Art Gilmore died at age ninety-eight on September 25, 2010. He and his wife, who survived him, had been married for seventy-two years.

ANTI-SELF-FUELING AIR ENGINES?
CARTOONIST FRANK BECK

Tacoma's jail at the end of the nineteenth century, a nine-year-old, two-story wooden building on South Twelfth Street, slightly east of A Street, was easy access for mischievous little boys. Just the right kind of place to jump up and down in front of the bars of a window and shout, "Oh, you crooks!" before running away. This was a favorite activity for future cartoonist Frank Beck and his friends. That is, until a rough-looking character popped up on the other side of the bars and shouted, "Take off your hat, son! Show a little respect or we'll look you up when we get out."

Frank Beck was born in 1893 in a log cabin near the boundary of Point Defiance Park. Eventually, his family moved closer to town, and Frank went to Bryant Grade School, then at 708 South Ainsworth. He also had a part-time job working for his contractor father, who was supervising some of the work involved in converting a badly burned hotel into what became Stadium High School. As a teenager, Frank was a delivery boy for the J.W. Fiddes Grocery Store. Fiddes's motto was: "We cater to good livers." Another job Frank had was at the Tacoma Smelting and Refining Company hammering blisters out of slab so it would pack down better.

When he wasn't working or at school, Frank loved to draw. At Stadium, he drew for the school's monthly newspaper, the *Tahoma*. He was listed as a staff artist on the yearbook along with J. Stedman Wood, who became a well-known artist in his own right. After graduation, Frank worked for a year on a ranch in Canada. Then, in 1912, he enrolled at the University of California–Berkeley, where he took mechanical drawing and studied to be an automotive engineer. However, he ran out of money and had to get a job. Later in life, Frank said that finding employment was pretty easy. Cadillac Motor Company hired him to work in its Detroit, Michigan advertising department. The job gave him time and money to attend classes at the Chicago Art Institute. At Cadillac, Frank specialized in designing car bodies. He also created the insignia—referred to as the Cadillac Crest—that is still used today. Frank served in World War I. During a temporary assignment at Camp Lewis, he drew cartoons for the camp's newspaper, *Trench and Camp*. After the war, he began his first cartoon strip, *Down the Road* (1920–36).

Classic Cadillac, circa 1907.

At that time, there was a little-known war going on within the automobile industry—the war to keep knowledge of air-run engines away from the public. Gasoline-driven engines were well established, and gas was cheap. Nevertheless, the general public loved air cars, or at least the idea of air cars. The self-filling air tank was around long enough for folks to discover what those early industrialists and air car inventors already knew: "air was tougher than stone, more plentiful than sunshine, cheaper than white bread and extremely powerful." Walt Disney drew a cartoon in which Goofy built a self-fueling air car, and Mickey mocked him for trying to "break the laws of thermodynamics." Mickey went on a ride with Goofy anyway, and the car crashed, but only because Goofy forgot to install brakes. Disney's assessment of the situation, put into the mouth of Goofy, was: "You can't stop it! Yuh can't stop air cars, because when people find out about them they will go hog wild!" (Presumably the people not the cars).

During this time period, from 1926 to 1937, Americans began reading Frank's daily cartoon, *Gas Buggie*. Also known as *Hem and Amy*, it depicted an obsessed man and wife "exercising ill-conceived delusions trying to invent an air car." Some readers wondered if Frank was creating subliminal, anti–air car messages.

One day, Frank met a *New York Tribune* executive who, seeing his work, said, "You ought to go to New York and be a cartoonist." Frank thought it was a job offer, so he quit his job and went east. When he arrived, the man explained that it had just been a comment. For a year and a half, Frank camped out on the fellow's doorstep. Eventually, he got a job as illustrator for the paper's automobile section.

Between 1935 and 1962, after cars stopped being new, Frank married, had a daughter and changed his cartoons to focus on family life. *All in a Lifetime* drew on their experiences. He also had a dog. By 1940, the cartoon was called *Bo*, and a dog became the central figure.

Frank had a collection of old ephemera about Tacoma and occasionally used bits and pieces for inspiration, sometimes including boyhood friends by name. He was usually six to eight weeks ahead of schedule, and on awkward occasions, his cartoons were published after a friend he mentioned had died.

The Becks lived in Canaan, Connecticut, and San Diego but regularly returned to Tacoma. Frank and his friends dined together either at the Winthrop Hotel or the Top of the Ocean. At one dinner, a three-layer cake was brought in, and using frosting tubes, Frank drew cartoons all over it.

During his peak years, Frank worked for the McNaught syndicate, and more than two hundred nationwide newspapers published his cartoons. At the time of his death, he was working on a series of books based on the cartoon strips and panels. He also had some deals in the works for a series of movies and a television show featuring talking dogs.

Frank Beck died in March 1962 before these ideas could come to fruition.

TINSEL TOWN IN TACOMA? THE WEAVER STUDIOS

Was ever a town luckier than Tacoma? An enormous natural harbor, miles of railroad tracks connecting the sails to the rails, seemingly daily announcements of a new skyscraper to be built, a beautiful mountain on the horizon that would have been called Mount Tacoma if not for some shenanigans pulled by Seattle involving the Board of Geographic Names and booze and then a Hollywood movie studio. It seemed as if there was no stopping the City of Destiny.

In 1924, H.C. Weaver formed H.C. Weaver Productions on five and three-quarters acres of land across the street from where Titlow Pool is today. It was the first movie studio in the Pacific Northwest. The main building of the studio was 105 by 180 feet with a 52-foot-high ceiling, a size considered adequate to allow three or four companies to work simultaneously under an abundance of klieg lights A separate administration building had executive offices, a projection room and fifteen dressing rooms for the stars and several others for lesser individuals. And there was one final amenity, a feature sure to entice other companies to use the Weaver studios facility: a developing laboratory. Right off the bat, four motion pictures were contracted.

Hollywood had come to Tacoma!

Hearts and Fists was the first movie made, and Tacomans were agog. The stars were John Bowers, who had recently appeared with Clara Bow in *Empty Hearts*, and Marguerite de la Motte, who was fresh from making *The Three Musketeers* with Douglas Fairbanks. However, before shooting could begin, the production unit had problems to work out. If the scene required white clothing, the clothes had to be dyed blue; white glared too much. Also, blue eyes photographed black. To counteract that, a prop man stood close to the actor but out of camera range and held up a piece of black cloth. Staring at it reduced dilation. Klieg lights lacked protective glass, and the arc threw off ultraviolet rays. Enough exposure and actors' eyes turned pink and swelled up. The first day's shooting of *Heart and Fists* was scheduled to begin at 9:00 a.m., but the dozens of arc lights and kliegs required two hours of additional adjusting. John Bowers appeared on time and fully made up but was worried about a hollow that showed up occasionally in his profile shots. He wanted the lights softened. And then there was costar Dan Mason's Van Dyke beard. To shave or not to shave? That was the question. Men wasted a full hour discussing the Van Dyke's fate. Finally, Mr. Weaver himself decided that Dan could keep his facial hair, which was really nothing more than a soul patch.

Indoor shooting finally began at 11:00 a.m. and went on all day. The outdoor shots were later done at Kapowsin.

The movie was about a successful lumber business Old Man Pond built but which had declined drastically while his son and heir, Larry, was away at college. Larry learns of a contract that, if filled, will save the business. The villain tries to force him out. Loyal employees step in to help. The movie ends with a logging train's race to get the timber to the mill while coping with burned-out bridges, loggers made intentionally drunk and a giant fir across the tracks. Larry marries the banker's daughter, and the villain is foiled.

Hearts and Fists premiered at Tacoma's Rialto Theater on January 22, 1926, and was released the next day. For the first time, a picture of the mountain and the words "Made in Tacoma" flashed on a motion picture screen.

The Totem Pole Beggar was next, but after "a psychological study," Mr. Weaver changed the title to the more evocative *Eyes of the Totem*. Wanda

On the set.

Hawley, Anne Cornwall, Gareth Hughes, Tom Santschi, Dan Mason (again), various local talent and the totem pole at the corner of South Tenth and A Streets starred. It's the story of an Alaskan woman and her child waiting for her husband's return from a prospecting trip. When he finally makes it back, he's murdered and robbed. Reduced to begging, the wife sits in front of a totem pole by which "all eyes must pass sooner or later."

According to the paper, "Everyone in Tacoma not working, and some who should have been" turned out to watch the filming, and at the end of the day, Wanda Hawley had been so convincing in her role that she had six copper pennies in her beggar's cup. "My dear daughter," she said to costar Anne Cornwall, "I'm afraid this won't send you very far through school."

Raw Country followed *Eyes of the Totem*. Anne Cornwall was back, and so was John Bowers, but the real star of the film was a team of sled dogs that achieved worldwide prominence during a race in 1925 to rush diphtheria antitoxin serum to Nome. The movie was their story.

For *Raw Country*, the production team built a Yukon town street scene at the studio. Tacoma resident J. Smith Bennett remembered that the buildings were all fronts supported by braces in the rear and that icicles were made of cotton dipped in melted paraffin. For real icicles and snow, outdoor action was filmed on Mount Rainier around Paradise Inn, Longmire and Narada Falls. During filming, a blizzard caught the cast unprepared. After a long wait, a break in the clouds let them see where they were in relation to the lodge. Safely back in front of a toasty fire, some members admitted to their fear, while others said they got some really wonderful views of the Tatoosh Range.

Other memories of these movies include the Winthrop Hotel's crystal ballroom made up as a cabaret, the tables filled with locals and the hotel's façade used as the exterior of a Chinese garden.

In May 1927, H.C. Weaver announced that the three movies would be released throughout the country by Pathe. However, *Raw Country* was distributed in the East under the name *In the Heart of the Yukon*, so no one would get the impression that it was "one of the usual wild westerns." It was released on May 29.

Alas, for H.C. Weaver, and for Tacoma, 1927 was the year Al Jolson made *The Jazz Singer*, the first talkie, and talkies led the inadequately equipped company into insolvency. The studio was converted into a ballroom. One night in August 1932, two men were seen leaving the premises. Shortly after, flames shot out of the structure. The caretaker and his wife barely escaped the fire, which destroyed all their belongings, including their car.

Automobiles lined both sides of Sixth Avenue for more than a mile; more than one thousand people watched a fire department, handicapped by lack of fire plugs, battle the blaze. In the end, all was destroyed.

After the fire, General James M. Ashton, legal representative for the Weaver concern, said the films had never been marketed. Researchers said that many of the old nitrate-based negatives failed to survive, these three included. As of this writing, it appears that *Eyes of the Totem* can be seen on the web. But if nothing else, the memories of people like J. Smith Bennett remain to herald a time described locally as a "Great Civic Event."

RISING TO THE OCCASION: LESSER-KNOWN VISITORS

Not all the famous or infamous people who traveled to the Pacific Northwest stopped at Tacoma. On their way to the Klondike, Wyatt Earp and his wife, Josie, skedaddled right on by Puget Sound, preferring a quick stop at Wrangell, Alaska. Mae West also skipped Tacoma when headed for British Columbia's Campbell River. And young women waited at the Union Depot for three days hoping that Clark Gable would make an appearance before going north to Mount Baker to make *Call of the Wild* with Loretta Young.

Nor was everyone who did visit Tacoma really famous except for short periods of time. David Warfield was a well-known American stage actor when he appeared at the Tacoma Theater in 1913 as the kindly old man in *The Return of Grimm*, a roll he created. Vaudeville actress

Lillian Russell at the height of her beauty.

Ethel Barrymore as she looked when she appeared in Tacoma.

Nell Kelly appeared on the RKO Orpheum with lesser-known Bob Hope in 1931. Martha Graham danced "in a modern extravaganza to soothe the savage beast" a few years later. Rod La Rocque helped open a new theater, and when John Phillip Sousa and his band traveled to Tacoma, the group needed special railroad cars for all the men and their equipment. Ethel Barrymore and Lillian Russell were both well received here, but Tacomans seemed to prefer Miss Russell, referring to her as having a "Juno-like stoutness"—a kind way of saying she was fat. The opera singer Madame Schumann-Heink was a particular favorite. Her oldest son, August, was in the German army during World War I, and she had three sons who were in the United States Navy, one who was a field artillery officer and her youngest son, Hans, who enlisted in the American cavalry. Both August and Hans died during the war, and Tacomans admired her courage as well as her talent.

Jumbo was a catalo, a cross between a buffalo and a cow. He and his human companion, L.C. "Buffalo Bill" Wilson of Colville, Washington, traveled more than 4,000 miles throughout the South and Northwest selling postcards to support themselves. However, Jumbo's trip was small potatoes compared to Rattlesnake Jim's 124,000-mile, around-the-world trek. Jim, whose real name was James Lauhno Lonefeather, was half Italian-Swiss and half Sioux. He didn't so much appear in Tacoma as he was found there, reading a Spanish dictionary and Latin grammar in the library's reference room.

Cowboy, comedian, humorist, vaudeville performer and social commentator Will Rogers flew here in 1927 and landed at the old Mueller-Harkins Airport. Rogers met with the mayors of Tacoma, Puyallup, Steilacoom, Centralia and Bucoda, and as he was the mayor of Beverly Hills, California, the men exchanged "freedom of my city" permits. Once these formalities were over, Rogers visited Camp Lewis, where silent screen star Richard Barthelmess was filming *The Patent Leather Kid*. Rogers was hugely popular at the time. His newspaper column full of wry observations ran in local papers. These days, he's mostly forgotten.

A number of visiting entertainers bought property in Tacoma. The famous American baritone David Bispham was one; so was Harry Houdini's brother, Ferencz Dezso Weisz (Houdini's real name was Erik Weisz). It was Ferencz, who went by the name of Hardeen, who came up with the idea of escaping from a straitjacket, a trick Houdini perfected. Sir Henry Irving, the first British actor to be knighted, made $17,000 by investing in property on C Street (now Broadway). Concert vocalist Madame Emma C. Thursby also invested in C Street property but forgot she owned it. When she discovered that her agent had sold the land without her permission, she sought legal advice and won, eventually netting herself a tidy profit. Stage actors Hans Robert and Max Figman and actress Henrietta Crosman all invested in Fircrest property.

Charlie Chaplin was billed only as "the clever English comedian" when he appeared with the Karno Company in a play called *The Wows Wows*. Johnny Weissmuller was just a swimmer when he appeared in a series of exhibition events at the Oakes on Steilacoom Lake. MGM star Jeannette MacDonald's career was on the wane when she and her dog, Stormy Weather, came on tour. However, Al Jolson had yet to make the *The Jazz Singer* when he was at the Tacoma Theater, and Billie Burke had not yet become known to the world as Glinda the Good in *The Wizard of Oz* when she visited friends Captain and Mrs. J.A. Toon.

Among Tacoma's more unique entertainers, conjoined twins Daisy and Violet Hilton were probably the most unusual. "Mayor Gets Two-Fisted Job (Handshake) When Introduced to Twins," the *Tacoma Daily Ledger* noted, adding that amongst their differences was the fact that Daisy liked to sew and Violet liked to cook. The sisters, born in 1908, were fused at the pelvis and buttocks; they shared blood circulation but no major organs. At the time, doctors felt it would be too dangerous to try and separate them. Their unmarried bartender mother, Kate Skinner, sold the girls to her boss, Mary Hilton. Hilton and her husband trained the girls to sing and dance and controlled them through abuse. They eventually died four or five days apart from Hong Kong flu. However, that was many years after the seventeen-year-old girls "offered song, dance, music and comedy" to Tacoma audiences.

Whether they were older, such as Lillian Gish and Basil Rathbone; still young, such as Johnny Sheffield; in the middle of their career, as was Mickey Rooney; or near the end, like Marjorie Rambeau, entertainers, politicians, writers and royalty came to Tacoma to entertain and in some cases be entertained. And a good time was had by all.

Part V

The Century Advances

Labor Speaks: The General Strike of 1918

The Russian revolution was planned in the office of a Seattle lawyer, counsel for the organization...during those three overheated days wherein Lenin and Trotsky tarried in the city's midst, enroute [sic] to Russia, an American revolution was planned or at least discussed at that time, it was evident that bolshevism has put forth its supremest [sic] effort in America and has failed.
—Saturday Evening Post

World War I and the burgeoning war industries brought an influx of laborers to Puget Sound that pushed up demand for everything from food to housing and strained utilities almost to the breaking point. Companies made huge profits by padding their shipping costs and sending large amounts of goods to Europe. But their greed resulted in shortages on the homefront. In three years, the cost of living rose by 50 percent, while at the same time workers saw their earning power decrease. Clearly, a situation was brewing.

At the time, Seattle had approximately thirty thousand shipbuilders and Tacoma about fifteen thousand. The men were members of the Metals Trade Union, part of the American Federation of Labor (AFL). However, the navy and most shipbuilding companies were organized under the United States Shipping Board. The shipping board had the power to set wages.

A strike is called.

Shortly after Germany's surrender, the board announced a nationwide, uniform wage scale for all shipbuilders.

Puget Sound laborers were incensed. If it was going to cost more to live here than in other parts of the country, and it did, and if local shipbuilding companies were willing to negotiate, and they were, union members felt there was no reason to submit to some sort of national wage scale that didn't take the cost of living differences into consideration. A local representative for the workers took their grievances to Washington, D.C. He returned with guarantees that the cost of living and wage negotiations would be given serious consideration. In reality, though, the Labor Adjustment Board's intent was quite different. In a telegram to the Metal Trades Association, the board's chairman said any company that raised wages beyond the set guidelines would be denied steel shipments—effectively putting them out of business.

By some strange "coincidence," Western Union "misdirected" the telegram to the Metal Trades Council's union. Once the union learned that the employers had no intention of negotiating, it called a strike. On January 21, 1919, shipbuilders in Tacoma and Seattle walked off the job. The Metal Trades Council then asked the Seattle Central Labor Council to call its members out on strike in a show of solidarity. One by one, unions and their members from many different industries—motion pictures projector operators, laundry workers, stage hands, allied painters' trades, longshoremen, smelter workers, carpenters—were drawn into the dispute. One hundred and ten unions had voted, and many of them voted to strike. A strategy committee agreed that a few bakeries, dairies and wholesale butcher shops could stay open to prevent suffering around town, but all the other food sources were to be closed so that everyone would see and recognize labor's power.

The Century Advances

Strikers were supposed to be fed at a commissary. Early morning of the first day, several thousand men and women milled around Tacoma's Labor Temple, waiting—and waiting and waiting. Those in charge underestimated the logistics of getting thousands fed. In the middle of the morning, bakery trucks began to arrive. Volunteers carried in loaves of bread and "stacked them like cord wood." Around noon, kettles of stew from a restaurant kitchen operating under commissary direction showed up. Two hours later, the doors opened, and people sat down to cold stew, chunks of bread and no silverware. After the first day, word went out that only the homeless would be fed.

In the meantime, the unions were busy forming a strike committee. The committee had the power to provide for auxiliary police and to decide which trades could continue to operate. For example: milkmen, yes; hearse drivers, yes; telephone operators, on standby basis only; janitors for the county and city buildings and labor temple, no.

Businesses in operation during the strike displayed placards stating that the business was operating with the approval of the General Strike Committee.

As the strike deadline neared, Tacoma became very quiet. Some people stockpiled supplies and stayed home. Streetcars stopped running. The armory at Eleventh and Yakima became headquarters for troops from Camp Lewis who, among other things, were sent to Tacoma to guard public utilities and maintain order.

In Seattle, the streets were also deserted. Unfounded rumors spreads: that the mayor had been assassinated, the water supply poisoned and power plants dynamited and that arson was rampant. Many wealthy residents left the state.

At the University of Washington, President Henry Suzallo called out ROTC students and told them to "save the world from the Bolsheviks." Although it was hardly revolt on a massive scale, a revolutionary spark did exist in Seattle, and both the strike leaders and government officials knew it. For that reason, union leaders ordered the rank and file to avoid crowds, and the *Union Record* was told to cease publication. Taking full advantage of the situation, Seattle mayor Ole "Holy Ole" Hanson got his picture "on the front page of most national newspapers and was featured in four national magazines."

Mayor Hanson immediately drew up plans for calling in troops to protect his city. Camp Lewis soldiers were already guarding reservoirs, power stations and various utility sights. But he wanted to secure shotguns and machine guns, stock up on ammunition and find additional places where soldiers could be stationed.

Tacoma laborers quickly decided that they'd been tricked into striking, and they quietly returned to work. Strikers in Seattle also figured out that because of governmental wage restrictions their actions accomplished nothing. With the loss of popular support, the strike ended rather ignominiously after five days—and five days' lost wages.

With the end of the strike, many workers had to reapply for their jobs, and not a few left the state. Mayor Hanson left the state, too. He resigned from his position, went on a nationwide lecture tour, wrote a book and tried to get himself nominated as the next Republican presidential candidate. He ended his days as a California real estate promoter. One man described Hanson as a man who, though "energetic and picturesque, said nothing in his speeches and accomplished even less—a Chamber of Commerce hero everywhere but in Seattle."

Meanwhile, Albert Johnson, a Washington State House representative, cried for deportations.

"There are five hundred Russians and Finns out there who ought to be started out of the country as soon as possible," he said.

For many years after the general strike, labor struggled. It seemed that every time the national government imposed cutbacks involving national contracts, the government saw to it that the Pacific Northwest got cuts before other parts of the country.

And though it irritated some and amused others, politicians of the time occasionally referred to "the forty-seven states and the Soviet of Washington."

LOOSE LIPS SAVED THE SHIPS

America hadn't even entered World War I yet when Jim Bashford, a veteran newspaper reporter covering Tacoma's waterfront, stumbled on a plot to blow up ships there and sabotage the docks. Had the plan succeeded, it would have been a rare act of unprovoked aggression perpetrated against the United States.

One day, as was his custom, Jim dropped by L. Benjamin's store on Pacific Avenue to see the waterfront regulars and call in to his newspaper. While doing these two things, he overheard a stranger say the word "Vladivostok." It struck Jim as odd, so he sidled up to the man and started a conversation. The man said he was headed to the Russian port and was making a few purchases for the trip. The reporter, however, knew that there was only one ship in the harbor, a British freighter, and it was highly unlikely that Vladivostok was its destination. So he asked the fellow what business he was engaged in, and the man lost his temper.

"My business is none of your damn business, my friend!" he snapped and left.

After a while, Jim also left Benjamin's and went to Olson's Tugboat Company. There he saw the stranger, chatting with George Marvin, a salesman for the DuPont Powder Company. Jim ducked out of sight, and after the man left, he asked George what the fellow wanted. George said that the stranger claimed to be a Pierce County chicken farmer and that he wanted to buy several hundred feet of fuse to use while blasting out some stumps. He was supposed to return later that afternoon.

Jim smelled a rat. He immediately contacted U.S. deputy marshal Ira Davison, and they staked out the tugboat office, but the stranger was a no-show. Two nights later, while riding at anchor outside Seattle Harbor, a scow loaded with dynamite was blown up.

Police officers from both Tacoma and Seattle went on a manhunt and arrested the supposed traveler to Russia. He was living on North Ferdinand and had no alibi. Unfortunately, none of the three law enforcement agencies involved had sufficient reason to detain him; also, there was some sort of dispute about what country owned the dynamited scow. And so the stranger was turned loose, and Jim Bashford forgot all about him—for a few months,

Boathouses on the waterfront. *Courtesy of Robin Paterson.*

anyway. Then Jim learned that the man had been arrested for trying to blow up a canal near Detroit. Bill Bryon, a U.S. Department of Justice agent, brought the man back to Tacoma, and he talked. He said he'd had big plans to blow up Tacoma's waterfront and industries and that, among other places, he'd hidden dynamite in some brush below Stadium Bowl and near the Northern Pacific Railroad's roundhouse. Jim and Agent Bryon found these two stashes. However, the big reveal came when the man implicated the German consul in San Francisco and Lieutenant Wilhelm Von Brincken, Germany's military attaché there.

But that wasn't all. He said that the schooner *Annie Larson* and the cargo steamer *Edna* had been surreptitiously loaded with ammunition and arms and had kept a rendezvous with German raiders operating in the Pacific. He also talked about a small Filipino steamer that had taken on cargo in Tacoma but had been held off Brown's Point because someone reported that a bomb was aboard. A search showed up nothing; the ship sailed away—and disappeared. No trace of it was ever found.

The stranger, whose name was never revealed, had one more secret. According to his sister, before he died, he told her that he had thrown the bomb during the Preparedness Day Parade that took place in San Francisco on July 22, 1916. This important-at-the-time-but-now-largely-forgotten parade was in anticipation of the United States' imminent entry into World War I. During the parade, a suitcase bomb was detonated, killing ten and wounding forty. Two men, Thomas Mooney and Warren Billings, were convicted in separate trials.

In a peculiar trick of fate, the accused Wilhelm Von Brincken was luckier. Although he did serve two years at McNeil Island, after being released, he went to Hollywood and made movies.

However, that wasn't Tacoma's only brush with terrorism. A few weeks after the United States entered the war, someone planted a five-gallon can of nitroglycerine on the ship *Saxonia*, in harbor for repairs. The 4.424-ton ship from the Hamburg-American line had been at Eagle Harbor, across the bay from Seattle. When the United States declared war on Germany, it was turned over to the navy. Shortly after the *Saxonia* docked, a navy man walking down the main deck saw the can and kicked it to see if it was empty. Realizing, from the sound, that it was full of something, the sailor sniffed it to see if it was gasoline. It wasn't, nor was it any other fuel that he recognized. He reported the matter to a superior officer, and as a matter of routine, government experts analyzed the contents and found pure nitroglycerine. It was immediately taken to the depot at Ostrich Bay in Kitsap County.

With safety ensured, what concerned the military was whether or not the can was placed on the ship as part of a foiled plot to blow it up. If so, in order to board the ship the individual had to be someone in either the government's or the military's confidence. Nothing was ever discovered.

Little has been written about World War I in the Pacific. The day before the *Saxonia* incident, two men at Fort Rosecrans in San Francisco reported sighting a submarine off the entrance to San Diego Bay, but sea and air investigations turned up nothing. Nevertheless, the commanding officer alerted other bases about the possibility of their existence. Historians now know that Germany was actively involved in trying to get the United States and Mexico in a war to divert the States from the European conflict. In 1917, the foreign secretary of the German Empire, Arthur Zimmermann, sent the Zimmerman Telegram to Heinrich von Eckardt, Germany's ambassador in Mexico. It was a diplomatic proposal from the German Empire encouraging Mexico to make war against the United States. The proposal was intercepted by British cryptographers, and the American press revealed its contents on March 1. The resulting outrage contributed to the United States' declaration of war against Germany in April.

Tacoma continued to be under Germany's eye. On April 8, 1918, several people saw a man named John Nagley standing on the bluff near Firemen's Park with pencil and paper in hand, either writing or sketching. At the time, the military police had rooms in the fire department headquarters. They were notified, and two military police officers went to arrest Nagley. When he saw them coming, Nagley tore up the paper and casually dropped it at his feet. The officers frisked Nagley and found a copy of the Morse code and another of the Continental code. The Continental, or International Morse code, as it was sometimes known, had been developed because radio telegraphic communication didn't work well with the early Morse code. It contained embedded spaces that were actually an integral part of several letters. The Continental code became the universal standard for Radio Telegraph Communications and for European land-line telegraphic communications. However, in America, railroad and intercity land-line telegraph operators continued to use the original Morse code until well into the 1960s. Getting back to Nagley, he also had a copy of the army's regulation code for flag signals and a code where Greek letters replaced letters of the alphabet. The men didn't find the scraps of paper until the following day. When they pieced them together, they saw a sketch with all the major bridges, warehouses and boatbuilding companies marked.

Nagley claimed to be a logger and an American, but he refused to explain the sketch or the codes he carried. Federal Secret Service special agent J.W. McCormick was called in, and Nagley was told he would probably be held for the duration of the war.

It was really thanks to alert residents that Tacoma was never attacked during World War I.

RAPID TRANSIT

Due to the danger of Spanish Influenza, all passengers and crew members are required to wear face masks to help prevent contagion. Anyone who refused to comply will be put off the train.
—Puget Sound Electric Company

In the days when land developers platted their property, laying out roads and putting in private streetcar lines, they did so with no obligation to connect them to those in the neighboring developments. That's the reason Tacoma has some peculiarly crooked streets. Nor did developers have an obligation to maintain the streetcar lines after the last plat was sold. The result of this, of course, was chaos.

In 1890, city officials hired the Boston firm of Stone & Webster to review Tacoma's transportation situation and make suggestions. The firm recommended that all the lines in Tacoma be owned and operated by one company and that the company build an additional line to connect Tacoma and Seattle. This concept immediately set up a battle over right of ways; people living along the Duwanish and White Rivers, for example, were served with notices that land along the proposed track that the company hadn't already acquired would be condemned. Claims for damages had to be presented in open court in Seattle on August 12, 1901. Other issues included control of timberlands, a source for the required electricity and stock and bond sales. It was ten years before the Puget Sound Electric (PSE) Company—or the Interurban, as it was known—was organized.

The PSE's intention was to provide top-of-the-line accommodations and service. The company hired the best streetcar operators from Seattle and Tacoma. The trains had Westinghouse's highest-quality airbrakes. Each passenger car accommodated sixty passengers and had wine-red upholstered seats and white linen headrests for their comfort. Each also carried its own

The Interurban.

tool kit for minor emergency repairs. Motormen were inaccessible to the riding population so as not to be disturbed while driving. Telephones dotted the tracks in case of major emergencies.

Passengers and people shipping commodities had twenty-three stops to consider. As many as twenty-five cars at a time made the run from Renton's brickyards and coal yards into Seattle. The Allentown quarry shipped crushed rock. Milk, meat and veggies were carried from valley farms into Seattle and Tacoma. And there were private excursions—to picnic grounds, Renton's Dance Pavilion or to Meadows Race Track near today's Boeing Field.

Tacoma's first train left the Seventh and A Streets terminal on September 25, 1902. A one-way trip from Tacoma to Seattle took about fifty-five minutes and cost sixty cents. Round trip was a dollar. The limited ran hourly and the local every two hours. The locals stopped at such bygone places as Sawmill, Stuck, Christopher, Thomas, O'Brien, O'Rilla, Black River, Argo and Flats. The trains were geared to run sixty miles an hour but could reach seventy miles per hour for short distances. Once, however, a train slipped its brakes at Milton and raced out of control down the hill into Tacoma. Neither passengers nor crew were willing to estimate its speed.

Over all, a trip on the Interurban was safe, though there were some incidents. The third rail, called the "Sleeping Monster" because of its high voltage, was responsible for the deaths of numerous wandering cows and horses. Snow, if sufficient to gather on the track, stalled the trains and caused the rail to flash and spark "like the Northern Lights." A tunnel through a sand hill near

Auburn occasionally caved in. Once, in a heavy fog, two trains collided on the Green River Bridge. Another time, a train ran a switch at Willow Junction (now Fife), injuring forty-two before it was brought under control.

However, regardless of its speed and efficiently, the Interurban was rarely profitable. A less-expensive boat service, which had been plying the waters between the two towns for years, provided keen competition. Only during the 1907–08 Alaska-Yukon-Pacific Exposition, when tourists made the trip to Seattle from all over Puget Sound, and during World War I, when the trains carried troops and shipyard workers back and forth between stations, did it make any money.

The trains and the rail system were a typical railroad in looks and function. But down on Tacoma's tide flats a Mr. William Boyles was experimenting with a more modern system. His cars had a streamlined nose to cut resistance and ran on a steel channel beam on top of a wooden beam supported by trestles, with side wheels running along the side of the beam. If that seems difficult to visualize, take a look at a modern monorail system.

Little is known about Boyle or his invention. It was apparently intended to run between Tacoma and Seattle, and Mr. Boyle had tried to sell stock in the venture. His prototype was a short-lived sight in 1911 and then disappeared.

The Interurban continued to operate, but even after a rate increase it lost money. And after twenty-six years of service, the roadbeds showed wear. When the ride was no longer comfortable, and automobiles became affordable, people took to the roads, and trucks took over the freight business. The PSE took an inventory and survey and decided that updating the equipment would be too expensive. The last train made its run on December 31, 1928. Railroad stations and waiting rooms were torn down and tracks taken up. Some of the old cars enjoyed second lives as restaurants, but they, too, were short-lived.

Now that there is a new rail system between Tacoma and Seattle, train aficionados can relish the fact that it was the availability of automobiles that "tooketh away" the original commuter trains, and it has been the sheer numbers of automobiles that caused their return.

WOMEN'S WORK

When manufacturing was local, Tacoma, like most mid-sized cities, was self-supporting. And many of the long-gone businesses speak of different interests and needs, especially women's work.

A lady and her apron.

Madsoe Manufacturing had a male CEO, Sydney Madsoe, but otherwise the company was created and run by women. Madsoe was born and raised in western Montana and came to Tacoma in 1937 for a change of climate and scenery. He had a background in marketing and store management and went to work at a Parkland market. From Parkland, he moved on to a store on South Thirty-eighth Street, where he had a chance encounter with Mrs. Freeda Wheeler. Mrs. Wheeler came in one day to see if she could sell some aprons she'd made.

"They were a good design and well made," Madsoe said, "and when I put them on display, they sold right away."

Madsoe was pleased with the interest homemakers showed in the aprons and asked Mrs. Wheeler to make more. Mrs. Wheeler not only made aprons, but she also made little girls' dresses. They, too, sold well. As a result, and in a really impulsive move, Madsoe quit his job and went into businesses with Mrs. Wheeler manufacturing aprons and dresses. He opened a shop at 1702 South K Street, with Mrs. Wheeler as the designer and superintendent of seven seamstresses who were piece workers; that is, each was paid by the number of items she finished in a day.

With twelve layers of cloth laid on a flat surface, employees cut out the pieces with electric scissors. They used colorfast print cotton or permanent finish organdy for the aprons. For the dresses, it was dotted Swiss, taffeta, rayon or crepe. The women did all the stitching but left the hems and buttonholes for a finisher to do. On an average day, each seamstress assembled thirty-five to forty aprons and somewhat fewer dresses.

Mrs. Wheeler was entirely self-taught but apparently very competent. Within two months, the Madsoe Company was shipping articles to shops in Montana, Idaho and Oregon. The business fit well in the female niche of the times.

It is difficult now to understand the value once placed on handmade lace. True lace is created when a thread is looped, twisted or braided to

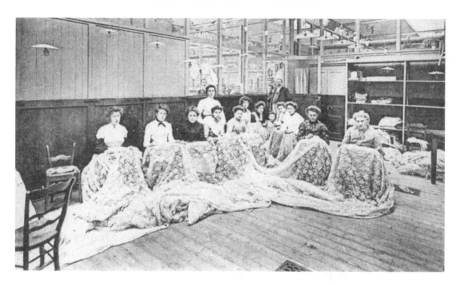

Showing off the lace.

other threads independent of a backing fabric. The oldest laces were made from linen, silk, gold or silver and are mentioned in pattern books as far back as 1540. Until lace-making machines largely destroyed the market for handmade lace, it was highly prized for its extraordinary beauty and intricate patterns and was considered to be quite a valuable item that only the wealthiest families could afford. Even after 1832, when cotton thread came along, people took particular care of their lace, constantly removing pieces from one item of clothing, washing it and stitching it onto others. But those people lucky enough to own lace curtains needed a professional to clean them, and in Pierce County that professional was Mrs. O.M. Yant.

In 1931, the *Tacoma Daily Ledger* had a series of articles it called "Old Timers on the Job." Most of the elderly people featured were men. Mrs. Yant was one of the few women. She lived at 342 Fifth Street in Puyallup and had a virtual monopoly on the cleaning and care of lace curtains. Even today, it's a fairly lengthy process and not an easy one because wet lace is more fragile than dry lace.

To clean old lace, Mrs. Yant soaked it in a tub of warm soap and water until the water was cool. Lace can shrink, so the water temperature is important. She repeated the process for twenty-four hours. When the lace seemed to be about as white as it was going to get, she rinsed it and laid it out flat on a towel, then rolled the towel up, pressing down carefully to get out the water. Then she unrolled the wet towel, transferred the lace to a dry one and left it flat to dry. Or, she put it on a tenter frame, which is a frame that allows fabric to dry evenly and in the right size. When the paper featured her as an "Old Timer still on the Job," Mrs. Yant was seventy-six.

In the days before Social Security, it was a frightening experience for a woman to unexpectedly have to find a way to earn a living. Mrs. Ethel Naubart Hamilton earned hers by converting a spare bedroom into a gift shop and selling items she made. Mrs. Hamilton learned the principles of design at Stadium High School and put what she'd learned to work in decorating fine Japanese and French china, some of which she sold to stores back east. She was a regular contributor to the monthly magazine *Keramic Studio*, contributed designs to various art schools and taught locally. When she wasn't designing and painting china, Mrs. Hamilton made dipped candies, lacquered baskets and rose potpourri.

Mrs. Lillian Stilton, on the other hand, made lavender sticks. When she moved to Tacoma from the east, lavender was a novelty to her. In 1910, she planted six cuttings, which fortunately for her thrived. Thereafter, every July she cut the blooms all at once, stripped off the leaves, divided the sticks according to length and quality and put them in her attic to dry. When she was ready to begin work, she put the sticks through a steaming process of her own invention to make them pliable. After that, she either made sachet bags or braided the stems with ribbons, pink and blue for babies or lavender for adults. In 1921, she made $500 and the following year, $1,000. She had standing orders from Rhodes Brothers Department Store in Tacoma, as well as stores in Seattle, Portland and Spokane and a few smaller towns. During an interview in 1922, she said that she didn't want to expand. She liked what she did; it kept her busy and provided a "fair-sized income."

Mrs. Charles Kuhn came to Tacoma from Vienna, where she was born and raised and where she learned the art of quilt making. Before Tacoma, she had lived in New York and worked for twelve years at Wanamaker's and Macy's department stores. When she and her husband came here, she found that there were no firms making down quilts, so she went into the business. Roughly every four months, a canvas sack of from two to four hundred pounds of grease-free eiderdown "plucked from the breast of live geese" arrived from Bohemia, which is how the Czech Republic was known. Each quilt took two and a half to three pounds of down, and the fabrics she used were silk or satin. A large portion of her quilts were hand-stitched, and she used her own designs and color combinations. In less than two years, she expanded and started making down pillows; she made them for adults, infants and dolls. One room in her home became a workroom, and a second room became a storeroom and showroom. She also had to hire two women to help with her business.

While these women were all doing well, Miss Agnes Joyce was having a harder time. Miss Joyce made paper flowers. All summer, she visited friends' gardens and the local parks and gathered samples to copy. At home, she dissected the blossoms to see how they were constructed and then copied nature. She made rose corsages, arrangements of marigolds and violets and mums for Thanksgiving and supplied hotels, private clubs, restaurants and homes. East Coast window trimmers used some of her paper flowers in yearly competitions. She was also interviewed for the newspaper and said that while she loved the work, there wasn't much money to be made—too much competition.

It was always difficult for a woman to go into business because she couldn't get financing in the way a man could. When Mrs. Westerdahl started Model Bakery at Thirty-eighth and Yakima, her husband did the baking, but she was the salesperson, the delivery person and everything else required to keep the business going.

Spinsters, widows and especially elderly women struggled just to be able to eat.

THE SUMMER OF '42: BOND DRIVES

Whether they were for raising money to help finance wartime military operations, to remove currency from an inflated economy or just to make people feel they were supporting the country's needs, United States Bonds played a vital role in World War II. However, the bonds didn't sell themselves. On June 9, 1942, when Tacoma was scheduled to kick off a major war bond drive, Mayor Happy P. Cain announced that actress Lana Turner was coming to help.

Miss Turner was one of MGM's defense bonds sales girls on loan by the studio to the U.S. Treasury Department. Prior to the announcement, she, her mother and her agent had been traveling up the Pacific coast, stopping at various towns along the way. When they reached Portland, Leon Titus, Pierce County's bond salesman, went down to Oregon and personally escorted the twenty-two-year-old starlet to Tacoma. During the trip, the party made official visits in Centralia, Chehalis, Toledo, Olympia and Tumwater and unofficial stops at other smaller towns. They arrived in Tacoma at 5:00 p.m.

WHAT DO YOU MEAN YOU WON'T BUY BONDS

Promoting bond drives.

and headed for the mayor's office in Old City Hall. There, Mayor Harry Cain pinned a corsage on the dark-colored suit Miss Turner wore and told her some important facts about the tide flats and waterfront. They posed for photographs, and then the actress hurried to her hotel to eat, bathe and change for a morale-boosting trip to Fort Lewis.

The next morning, a 1924 Lincoln Touring car, sporting a large flag, picked up the actress and took her to the Seattle-Tacoma Shipbuilding Corporation for an 11:30 a.m. appearance. She wore a white short-sleeved dress with a small black print and a black hat with a brim so big it blocked out backgrounds in many photographs. Nevertheless, in thirty minutes she sold $94,545 worth of bonds, giving kisses to men who bought them in the largest denominations. Then it was back to Tacoma for a big sales rally at Liberty Square.

Liberty Square, a small building built in the middle of two lanes of Tenth Street and Pacific Avenue, was still under construction. Miss Turner addressed the crowd from a bandstand, saying that many of the virile young bond buyers could kiss just as well as Clark Gable. At the end of her speech, a band started playing swing music, and the actress went to work selling bonds and signing each one so the buyer would have an autograph. Mayor Cain stood nearby chanting, "Buy bonds, buy bonds."

A huge crowd gathered. Children climbed onto rooftops and created so much racket that police officers ended up chasing them down the fire escape ladders. While this was going on, Miss Turner sold $120,000 worth of bonds, the highest denomination being $500. Then, after several hours in the City of Destiny, she left for stops in Seattle, Spokane, Coulee City and her birthplace, Wallace, Idaho.

Hot on Miss Turner's bond-selling trail came child star Johnny Sheffield, well known for his role as Boy in the Tarzan movies. Johnny was traveling with his mother and a tutor, and for whatever reason, Mr. Titus didn't see the need to meet him at the Oregon/Washington border. However, once Sheffield was in Tacoma, he did feign terror in the presence of the "boy of the jungle," pretending fear of a physical assault by Tarzan Jr.

Lana Turner's slogan was: "Over the top with bonds." For ten-year-old Sheffield, who wore a Boy Scout uniform and arrived at Liberty Square with a thirteen-ton army tank, it was: "Buy tanks for Yanks."

Nineteen-year-old starlet Linda Darnell came on July 11. Hometown boy Bing Crosby paid a visit on August 4. Workmen completed the Liberty Square building just in time for a Labor Day dedication on September 8 and a visit by British actress Joan Leslie, American actor Adolphe Menjou and Canadian actor Walter Pigeon.

Their day began at 10:00 a.m. with the obligatory stop at the mayor's office, followed by an 11:00 a.m. visit to the Seattle-Tacoma Shipyards, where they put on a program. After lunch, they joined a crowd of ten thousand at Liberty Square. Miss Leslie addressed the spectators, and Menjou held a mock soldier-dressing stunt, asking onlookers to buy bonds to help outfit a private. One man bought $500 worth of bonds to provide the soldier with a right foot boot; another spent $400 for a belt buckle. A bayonet and other required pieces of apparel eventually cost the crowd $23,635. However, Walter Pigeon was the hit of the day. As a former stock-and-bonds broker, he talked about knowing a good investment when he saw it. City officials made speeches and read congratulatory telegrams from various Washington, D.C. officials, and the Fort Lewis band provided music. At 3:30 p.m., the stars attended a ship launching and reception and then left for Seattle. The next day, the *Tacoma News Tribune* announced record sales of $509,095.

After the war, there were plans to move the Liberty Square building to 800 Broadway, but the idea fell apart; it was demolished instead. Fading memories and possibly an autograph or two are all that's left from Tacoma's summer of '42.

Bibliography

Ambrose, Mary J. Family history. March 15, 1978.

Ambrose, Samuel. Advertising letter with photographs and descriptions.

———. *The Ambrose Clover Creek Sanitarium*. Biennial report, 1918.

———. *The Highway to Health: Speed Laws*. N.d.

———. Letter from the Dr. Ambrose Sanipractice Institute, February 28, 1928.

Bergman, Hans. *A History of Scandinavians in Tacoma and Pierce County*. N.p.: Bergman, 1926.

Blackwell, Alice. *Reminiscences of Tacoma*. Tacoma, WA: Tacoma Public Library, 1911.

Blackwell, Ruby Chapin. *A Girl in Washington Territory*. Washington State Historical Society, July 10, 1973.

City Planning Commission. *Outline of a Master Plan for Tacoma: A Preliminary Report*. Tacoma, WA, December 1947.

Department of Community Development. *Glimpse at Tacoma's History*. Report, 1980.

Forslund, Stephen J. *The Swedes in Tacoma and the Puget Sound Country, 1852–1976*. Edited by Doris Gundstrom King. N.p., 1976.

History of Pierce County. Vols. 1 and 3. N.p.: Heritage League of Pierce County, 1990, 1992.

Hunt, Herbert. *History of Tacoma*. Chicago: S.J. Clarke, 1916.

Konzo, Seichi. "Far Away and Long Ago." Bank of California, 1977.

BIBLIOGRAPHY

More Than a Century of Service: The History of the Tacoma Police Department. Tacoma Police Department, 2009.

Morgan, Murray. *Puget's Sound: A Narrative of Early Tacoma and the Southern Sound.* Seattle: University of Washington Press, 1979.

Reese, Gary Fuller. *Did It Really Happen in Tacoma? A Collection of Vignettes of Local History.* Tacoma, WA: Tacoma Public Library, 1975.

Ripley, Thomas Emerson. *Green Timber.* New York: American West Publishing Company, 1968.

Swan, James G. "Closing the Frontier, 1853–1916." In *Northwest Passages: A Literary Anthology of the Pacific Northwest from Coyote Tales to Roadside Attractions.* N.p.: Sasquatch Books, 1994.

Weightman, Gavin. *The Frozen Water Trade: A True Story.* New York: Hyperion Books, 2003.

Wiley, Martha. "South Tacoma." In *History of Pierce County, Washington.* Dallas, TX: Taylor Publishing Company, 1990.

Wynbrandt, James. *The Excruciating History of Dentistry.* New York: St. Martin's Press, 1998.

NEWSPAPERS

News Tribune
New York Times
Puyallup Valley Tribune
Seattle Times
Senior Scene
Tacoma Daily Ledger
Tacoma Daily News
Tacoma Herald
Tacoma Times

INTERNET REFERENCES

www.brewerygems.com/histories.htm
www.cityoftacoma.org
www.etext.virginia.edu/railton/onstage/world.htm

BIBLIOGRAPHY

www.historylink.org

www.plu.edu/archives/sie/Oral-History-Collections/home.php

www.scribd.com/doc/29005616/Compressed-Air-Conspiracy-Timeline-
    Pt-1-4pp

www.tacomapubliclibrary.org

www.tysto.com/articles06/q4/20061017hats.shtml

wikipedia.org/wiki/Preparedness_Day_Bombing

About the Author

Karla Stover graduated from the University of Washington with honors in history. She has been writing for more than twenty years. Locally, her credits include the *Tacoma News Tribune*, the *Tacoma Weekly*, the *Tacoma Reporter* and the *Puget Sound Business Journal*. Nationally, she has published in *Ruralite* and *Birds and Blooms*. Internationally, she was a regular contributor to the *European Crown* and the *Imperial Russian Journal*. In addition, she writes two monthly magazine columns. In 2008, she won the Chistell Prize for a short story entitled "One Day at Appomattox." Weekly, she talks about local history on KLAY AM 1180, and she is the advertising voice for three local businesses. Her book *Let's Go Walk About in Tacoma* came out in August 2009. She is a member of the Tacoma Historical Society and the Daughters of the American Revolution. Her entire working career was at Merrill Lynch.

Visit us at
www.historypress.net

CPSIA information can be obtained
at www.ICGtesting.com
Printed in the USA
LVHW081928210119
604680LV00011B/268/P